HISTORY OF THE LEGAL STATUS OF THE AMERICAN INDIAN

WITH PARTICULAR REFERENCE TO CALIFORNIA

A Thesis

University of Southern California

By

Donald R. Beatty

1957

Reprinted in 1974 by

R AND E RESEARCH ASSOCIATES

4843 Mission St., San Francisco 94112

18531 McFarland Ave., Saratoga, CA 95070

Publishers and Distributors of Ethnic Studies

Editor: Adam S. Eterovich

Publisher: Robert D. Reed

Library of Congress Card Catalog Number

74-76497

ISBN

0-88247-254-2

INTRODUCTION

Since the first white men landed in this hemisphere the problem of how to handle the Indians has been of prime importance. Consistently the laws have decreed one way of treatment, and the actual practice of treating with the Indian in the field has been different. In many instances the Spanish, Portuguese, English, French, and Americans have despoiled and murdered the Indians.

In this study the writer is interested in the laws and statutes that have been promulgated by the different countries involved as they relate to the Indians of this hemisphere historically, and reflect on the treatment of the Indians of California and their status today.

To accomplish this aim it may seem that in some instances we are going a short way afield, but to gather in the loose threads of this study digressions were necessary. They are not really digressions because learned theologians, lawyers, popes, emperors, captains-general, dictators, presidents, cortes, congresses, and a host of other groups and individuals have made up the body of laws that are extant covering the governing of the Indians. Several times there have been efforts to help the Indian approach the civilization that the white man enjoys. Always some deterrent has arisen to discourage the progress that may have been made. Thus the problem has been carried down to our day. In 1933 and 1934 the first comprehensive steps were taken to alleviate the conditions under which the Indians exist in the United States.

Only a small beginning has been made in the years since the Indian Reorganization Act. There seems to be an endeavor afoot to implement the full integration of the Indian into our society now. Apparently the current answer is that Indians are citizens with all the rights, privileges and responsibilities thereunto pertaining; but, above and beyond this, they have certain additional protections due to their wardship status. The result is that now, theoretically, the Indian is in a more favored position than the white man as far as legal status is concerned. The courts have found no incompatibility between being both a citizen and a ward at the same time.

The problem of the legal status of the Indians is an extensive topic. Only the overview of so large a problem can be taken. In this study the writer has made an effort to touch upon many of the key points without intensive investigation of all the interesting facets of the problem which have presented themselves during the course of this investigation.

TABLE OF CONTENTS

CHAPTER I

LEGAL STATUS OF THE INDIAN UNDER SPAIN

AND MEXICO, 1492-1848

In the initial stage of the rule of the Spanish Crown it was the oft
reiterated wish and command of Queen Isabella I that the Indians were to be
free from servitude. It was further commanded that they were to be molested
by no one, and they were to be allowed to live free, governed in equal justice
as vassals of Castile.[1]

It was unfortunate for the American Indians that Isabella died so soon
after the discovery of the New World. After the rule was assumed by Ferdi-
nand V, as Regent, the Carib Indians were all but exterminated under one
pretext or another. Usually it was claimed they were cannibals, and as such
had no rights. This set a pattern for the treatment of Indians that has not yet
run its full course.

The near extermination was facilitated in those early times by the
application of the _repartimiento_ which allowed the Indians to be taken any-
where in the New World to perform any task demanded of them. Quite liter-
ally, under the governorship of men like Bobadilla, the Indians were worked
to death.

By command of the Regent, through the Law of Burgos, promulgated
December 12, 1512, it was ordered:

> That the persons who had Indians allotted (_encomendados_) to them,
> should build homes for them, called _bohios_, and supply them with
> provisions; that, when the houses were built, those which the Indians
> had in their own settlements should be burnt, so that they might lose
> the longing to return to them; and that in this removal violence should

not be used to them, but much gentleness. It was decreed that Churches should be built, provided with images and ornaments . . . .[2]

The Laws of Burgos merely substituted the _encomienda_ for the _repartimiente_. All that the greater defender of the Indians, Bartolome de las Casas, could do to intervene between the Indians and the Emperor, Charles V, alleviated the plight of the Indians little. Las Casas made at least four trips across the Atlantic to place the case of the helpless Indians before the Emperor. He tried to cast into disrepute the systems of _repartimiento_ and _encomienda_. He bitterly attacked the _caciques_ who made gains through the misery of their fellow men, and the _alcaldes_, inspectors, _corregidores_, _regidores_ and _ayuntemiento_ councils introduced by the Spaniards to keep closer hold upon the Indians.[3]

In 1532 the emperor sought advice in treating the Indians of America. He wanted to know how much of their consent he should have in the cessions of land and changes in political status. His choice as advisor was Franciscus de Victoria, an eminent lawyer-priest. Victoria carefully weighed the arguments of the day. The Indians of the New World were considered by a wide circle of learned men to be barbarians who, by committing of the sin of unbelief and other sins, could not own land. Even at this early time there was talk of the Indians being of unsound mind because they were Indians. His ultimate decision was that the Indians were the real owners before, and after, the advent of the Spaniards. He further held that the discovery of the lands by Europeans did not vest any title in the discoverers. Any seizure on the pretense that the land had been ownerless, or that some operation of the divine right of king or pope gave such right was in error. Appropriation of the land by any form of warfare was invalid. Only the voluntary consent of the Indian in the giving up of his land would create a valid transfer of title. The learned doctor of law and theology went even further and stated that the internal government of the Indians was to be respected by the invading Spaniards. Here again he allowed that the Indians might consign their rights of government to the Spaniards. The emperor read the findings of the good lawyer-priest, but he did not carry out the legal advice he had sought and obtained. There was nothing to stop the Spaniards in the Americas from claiming that the Indians had given them their land and rights to govern.[4]

On June 4, 1537, Pope Paul III issued the Bull Sublimis Deus. In this Papal Bull the highest authority in the Church of Rome determined that the Indians of the West Indies were human beings. We could afford a chuckle over this if it were not for the fact that there are undoubtedly people in the world today who still question the humanity of the Indian. In his Bull Pope Paul stated:

> The enemy of the human race, who opposes all good deeds in order to bring men to destruction, beholding and envying this, invented a means never before heard of, by which he might hinder the preaching of God's word of Salvation to the people: He inspired his satelites who, to please him, have not hesitated to publish abroad that the Indians of the West and the South, and other people of whom we have recent knowledge should be treated as dumb brutes created for our service, pretending that they are incapable of receiving the catholic faith.

> We, who, though unworthy, exercise on earth the power of our Lord and seek with all our might in bringing those sheep of His block who are outside, into the fold committed to our charge, consider, however, that the Indians are truly men and that they are not only capable of understanding the Catholic faith but, according to our information, they desire exceedingly to receive it. Desiring to provide ample remedy for these evils, we define and declare by these our letters, or by any translation thereof signed by any notary public and sealed with the seal of any ecclesiastical dignitary, to which the same credit shall be given as to the originals, that, notwithstanding whatever may have been or may be said to the contrary, the said Indians and all other people who may later be discovered by Christians, are by no means to be deprived of their liberty or the possession of their property, even though they be outside the faith of Jesus Christ; and that they may and should, freely and legitimately, enjoy their liberty and the possession of their property nor should they be in any way enslaved; should the contrary happen, it shall be null and of no effect.[5]

Hernando Cortes and his little band of Spaniards were thoroughly conversant with the operation of the encomienda system. Indeed few of the gentlemen from Spain, no matter how base born he might have been, wanted to dig in the soil or labor in the mines. As long as the Indians were at hand their labor was impressed to do the hard and menial tasks.

In 1542 the New Laws were enacted which decreed that all encomiendas would cease at death of the holder, and no new ones were to be granted. Slavery was to be abolished; and the laws were to be published in the Indian languages. In Peru the viceroy was killed by Spaniards when he attempted to put the New Laws into effect.[6]

The emperor had ordered the freeing of the Indians, but his orders were disobeyed because to free the Indians might have meant the withdrawal of the Spaniards from the New World. Six hundred colonists sailed from Vera Cruz on the next fleet after Francisco Tello de Sandoval had read the provisions of the New Laws. The colonists had come to the Americas to improve their lot and they felt they needed the labor of the Indians. It was further feared that unless the Spaniard kept the Indian subservient their numerical superiority would force the withdrawal of the white man.[7]

Viceroy Antonio de Mendoza (1535-1551) was an example of the finer type of Spanish official.[8] It was during his administration that action was taken to retain the Indian system of communal life and law, and the recognition of the personal rights of the Indian. Before the Spaniards came the Indians of New Spain lived in their calpulli, a clan formation. It has been the aim of Indian reformers since Mendoza to return the Indians to the calpulli type of organization.

Through the clever manipulation of the laws of Spain, or the outright breaking of the Spanish law, the white man stripped the Indians of the New World. In spite of the laws forbidding violation of the person and property of the Indians, the passivity of the military and ecclesiastical hierarchy during much of the Colonial Period permitted the violations expressly prohibited by law. The frightful conditions ensuing from the degeneration of the quality of the high officers sent to Mexico by the kings of Spain were felt most tragically by the Indians.

With the advent of Charles III to the Spanish throne there was a reflection of his absorption with the French concepts of administrative efficiency and purity. Charles reigned from 1759 to 1788, and during this time he sent Jose de Galvez as Visitor-General and Antonio Maria Bucareli as Viceroy to Mexico. The personal sufferings of the Indians were much alleviated during the regimes of Galvez and Bucareli. For their time and position these two men were far advanced. Revilla Gigedo followed Bucareli as Viceroy of Mexico, and even with him peace and prosperity, relatively speaking, were the catchwords of the time. In the year 1794 Revilla Gigedo was recalled and from that time on the quality of viceroys deteriorated. This situation endured until Iturbide led the armies of revolution against the Spaniards and won the independence of Mexico from Spain.

The Plan of Iguala, promulgated on February 4, 1821, did very little for the Indians directly, but as a statement of equality it has always been basic to Indianismo in Mexico. It had as its basis three guarantees:

a. Mexico was to be an independent monarchy under some European prince;

b. the Roman Catholic Church was to retain its privileges;

c. and all of the inhabitants of New Spain were to be citizens of this fine new monarchy.

All the inhabitants of New Spain, without distinction, whether Europeans, Africans, or Indians are citizens of this monarchy, with a right to be employed in any post according to their merits and virtues.[9]

This Plan has had a great deal of importance as a rallying point for the theory that Indians of California, for instance, were citizens of Mexico while Mexico ruled here; and in accord with the provisions of the Treaty of Guadalupe Hidalgo became citizens of the United States and the State of California.

Echavarri, General under Emperor Iturbide, accomplished nothing for the Indians in his Plan of Casa Mata of February, 1823. The new republic set up in 1824 under the presidency of Guadalupe Victoria did one thing for the Indians under Mexican rule--the Indian tribute was abolished. The effect on the Indians of far off California was nil.

It has been argued as a point in law that an Indian in California whose ancestors dwelt here were not inhabitants in the literal sense of the word as meant in the Plan of Iguala. The word habitantes in the Plan of Iguala does not mean inhabitant as the modern translator has construed the word; but means a settled person and not nomadic peoples. In cases before various courts of the Southwest it has been questioned whether the promulgators of the Treaty of Guadalupe Hidalgo had the ancestors of the present day Indians in mind when they wrote "Mexican now established."[10]

According to the Treaty of Guadalupe Hidalgo formally exchanged between Mexico and the United States at Queretaro on May 30, 1848, Article VIII declares:

> Mexicans now established in territories previously belonging to Mexico, and which remain for the future within the limits of the United States, as defined by the present Treaty shall become citizens of the United States if they remain in such territory for one year without declaring their intention to retain Mexican citizenship.[11]

In view of the facts pointed out by A. L. Kroeber which lead to the evidence that many tribal groups have lived in narrowly confined pieces of land in California for hundreds, and perhaps thousands of years, it would seem that the Indians of California are habitantes in almost any respect the word can be translated.[12]

The Spaniard came to California and found the Indians in their native state. It seems that their attitude was one of paternalism. The Indian was treated like a wayward, or rather, a backward child who had to be trained in the way of life that led to industry and godliness. The Padres came and with the aid of the military established their missions for the purpose of training the Indian. As time passed the colonies of the Americas revolted against the dominion of the mother country, Spain. The Mexican hold on California was rather tenuous and interlopers began to appear. The man who came by overland routes were interested in trapping, and at first gave the Mexicans little trouble. Those coming by sea were strong and aggressive men who sought fame and fortune, and California was the place to find those things. With them ideas of paternalism toward the Indian were not popular.

Legally, under the Patronato Real (Royal Patronage), the King of Spain was granted secular administration of the Church in the New World. Through the Royal Patronage the Pope had granted the King and his delegated rulers appointive rights to positions within the Church. Under the laws of Spain the system of missions in the New World was established to change the Indians from pagan to Christian, Spanish style.[13]

Entry into mission life was on a voluntary basis. Indians were induced to submit to the restraining influence of mission life by various means. But, once an Indian had become a neophyte he could not leave the mission until the government gave legal permission. Legal permission to leave the mission and become a free Indian was a mixed blessing because the free Indian was obligated, by law, to pay the annual tax tribute.[14]

Theoretically the missions belonged to the Indians, but the friars ruled with supreme authority. There was an actual enslavement of the bodies of the Indians by the missionaries to facilitate the salvation of their souls. If an Indian was foolish enough to attempt escape from the physical labor and spiritual exercises he was compelled to do, he was tracked down and returned to his mission by the military guard. Reprisals for attempt at escape and other infractions were harsh and unrelenting. Punishment was in the hands of native petty officials and the corporal of the guard on order of the missionaries.[15]

Spanish law declared that the mission should be considered successful and secularized after a period of ten years. This disbanding of missions and transformation to civilian towns was never attempted in California under Spanish rule. Here the Indian remained in paternalistic slavery throughout the Spanish Period, which ended in 1822. The Spanish Cortes (1813) decreed emancipation of the Indians and immediate secularization of all missions which had been in existence for ten years or more but it was 1821 before the law of 1813 was heard of in California, and it was ignored.[16]

The government of Mexico promulgated the Spanish Cortes Law of 1813 in 1821. Governor Echeandia issued a decree of secularization in California on July 25, 1826. No real action was taken in the area to implement secularization until 1831. When Figueroa arrived in California as the new governor he was forced to order the secularization of ten missions in a proclamation of August 9, 1834. In 1835 six more missions were secularized, and in 1836 the last five missions were secularized.[17]

Despite the law which proclaimed the land to be the property of the Indians there took place a rapid disposal of the land to Californians. The Indians either remained in virtual slavery on the secularized mission property, returned to their previous state of barbarianism, became drifters and loafers, or labored on ranches in the lowest possible status.[18]

Before the possession of the ranches in California changed from the Mexicans to the Americans old Spanish regulations governing land-holdings usually contained clauses for the protection of the Indians on the land. After the Americans took over the state, the Indians were driven into the desert and non-productive areas.[19]

FOOTNOTES

[1] Henry Stevens, A Facsimile Reprint of the Original Spanish Edition of the Cedulas and New Laws of the Indies (London: Chiswick Press, 1893, Private Printing), p. lxix. [Huntington Library folio.]

[2] Stevens, op. cit., p. lxxii.

[3] Herbert Ingraham Priestley, "Spanish Colonial Municipalities," California Law Review (Berkeley: University of California Press, 1919), pp. 397-416.

[4] Felix S. Cohen, "Original Indian Title," Minnesota Law Review, XXXII (1948), 40-44.

Franciscus de Victoria, professor at Salamanca (De Indis II, 6), (De Indis III, 10). James Brown Scott, former Solicitor for the Department of State and President of the American Institute of Law, American Society of International Law, and the Institute de Droit International, in his brochure on the Spanish Origin of International Law (1928), comments: "In the lecture of Victoria on the Indians, and in his tractate on War, we have before our very eyes, and at hand, a summary of the modern law of nations." The Seventh Pan-American Conference, on December 28, 1943, acclaimed Victoria as the man "who established the foundations of modern international law."

See Felix S. Cohen, "The Spanish Origin of Indian Rights in the Law of the United States," Georgia Law Journal, XXXI (1942), p. 1.

[5] Cohen, "Original Indian Title," pp. 45-46.

[6] F. A. MacNutt, Batholomes de Las Cases: His Life, His Apostolate, and His Writings (Translated 1909), pp. 429-431.

[7] Henry Banford Parkes, A History of Mexico (Boston: Houghton Mifflin Company, 1950), pp. 91-95.

[8] Parkes, loc. cit.

[9] United States v. Ritchie, 58 U.S. 525, 538; also see Parkes, op. cit., pp. 166-188.

[10] United States v. Santistevan, 1 N.M. 583, 591.

[11] Anderson v. Mathews, 174 Cal. 537, 542-4.

[12] A. L. Kroeber, Handbook of the Indians of California (Berkeley: California Book Co., 1953), p. 939.

[13] John Walton Caughey, California (New York: Prentice-Hall, Inc. 1953), pp. 71-86.

[14] Charles E. Chapman, A History of California: The Spanish Period (New York: Macmillan Company, 1921), pp. 150-155.

[15] loc. cit.

[16] Caughey, loc. cit.

[17] Loc. cit.

[18] Edward Everett Dale, The Indians of the Southwest (Norman: The University of Oklahoma Press, 1949).

[19] Rockwell D. Hunt, A Short History of California (New York: Thomas Y Crowell Co., 1929).

CHAPTER II

LEGAL STATUS OF THE INDIAN DURING EARLY

AMERICAN CONTROL, 1848-1865

To the east of California the years between 1821 and 1848 produced
a great migration of citizens of the United States to the Mexican territory of
Texas. Both Presidents Polk and Tyler were committed to the glorious dream
of "Manifest Destiny" of the United States. The prime direction in which this
destiny could logically aim was into lands owned by Mexico. It has been set
forth that the settlers in Texas came for a place to expand and carry on slavery without fear of hindrance. In the Mexican areas it was possible to hold
large grants of land in excess of the acreage allowed in the United States.
This was no doubt a factor in moving many Southern plantation owners from
their worn-out lands. It is possible that some politicians in the midst of the
newcomers did come with the hope that the additional land would maintain the
balance of power in Congress that the increased immigration from overseas
was disturbing in the favor of the Northern States.

As carefully as the other interests were to mask their intentions of
following through to the Pacific in a grab for land, the Mexicans seem to have
been aware of what was transpiring. Texas declared her independence from
Mexico in 1836, but the United States Congress failed to ratify annexation to
the Union until 1845. Mexico went to war with the United States which ended
in the defeat of the Mexican forces and the seizure of Mexico City by United
States forces. Nine days before the treaty between the United States and
Mexico was signed, gold was discovered in California. When the treaty was
ratified no one east of the Sierra Nevada knew of the discovery. Needless to
say the discovery of gold in California changed the entire pattern of all life

in California. It was one of the most important single events occurring within the nineteenth century in the world. It is doubtful whether any relatively unpopulated area on the face of the earth had ever been so heavily peopled in so short a time. States to the east of California were admitted to the Union after a long, slow formation through a frontier stage followed by a territorial stage which eventually developed into statehood. The different institutions that we ascribe to the growth of population gradually over many years, such as stable political organizations and religious bodies with roots sunk deeply, did not have time to form in California. Years of organized territorial government are not to be had here, and the Constitution of 1849 was a stereotype of the existing constitutions in the middle west and east. Wide powers were left to the legislature. Rapid changes in the population and industrial pattern about the state were not hindered by the loose fabric of the first constitution.

The Indians that the Padres had earlier gathered into the Mission system, and who were known as the Mission Indians, were in the way of the whites who poured into the state after 1848. Even if the Mission Indians had not physically been in the way, they would have had to be eliminated to obtain the rich lands upon which the Franciscan Fathers had placed a deed of trust for the Indians. Through the mixture of Spanish, Mexican, and Anglo-Saxon law, with a little mixture of outlaw, the land was simply delivered from the weak to the strong.[1] The excuse has been advanced that after the diggings began to give out the newcomers began to seek land upon which to settle, and the lands that the Missions had been on were in the center of things and had the finest soil.

The California Indians had been numerous, but they had very primitive cultures. The feeling toward the Indians can be illustrated in an order of the day issued by a military commander to the alcalde of one of the pueblos authorizing the shooting of Indians on sight caught stealing horses. Indians that were employed by whites were issued a word card. Indians without work certificates were to be arrested and punished as vagrants.[2]

The fact that the Mexican laws of secularization had ordered Mission lands to be distributed to the Indians living on the land made little difference to the whites coming into the fertile areas of Southern California. The property of the Indian was supposed to be his own by law but the laws were ignored.[3]

The simple equation that the principle of Roman law was employed in California will not stand up under the rules of equity, but it has been advanced. The principle is that the finder of ownerless chattel obtains title to the chattel by having made the discovery and done something about the discovery. The arguments that might be advanced today that the Indians were free men before the Americans came; and the doubt as to whether there was a discovery of ownerless chattel under the provisions of the laws of Spain and Mexico and in accord with the Treaty of Guadalupe Hidalgo are mere rhetoric in retrospect, and they were ignored in the mid-nineteenth century period.

During the early American occupation of California the Indian was so little considered and his rights denied to such an extent that in no case could a white man be convicted of any offense upon the testimony of an Indian or Indians. In all cases it was discretionary with the court or jury after hearing complaint of an Indian as to what steps should be taken.[4] This was the measure of the rights then of the Indian as against the rights of the white man with whom he dealt.

Hubert Howe Bancroft put it most succinctly when he wrote of the resolving of the California Indian Policy:

> That part of the early intercourse between aboriginal Americans and Europeans which properly belongs to history may be briefly given. For short work was made of it in California. The savages were in the way; the miners and settlers were arrogant and impatient; there were no missionaries or others present with even the poor pretense of soul-saving or civilizing. It was one of the last human hunts of civilization, and the basest and most brutal of them all.[5]

General Stephen W. Kearny maintained and showed a friendly attitude toward the Indians while he was the Military Governor of California. He wished to retain their good will be distributing presents among them. His successor, Governor Richard B. Mason, shared his desire and urged the reclamation of the Mission Indians who had fled into the mountains and deserts. There was a relative peace from the time of General Kearny's conquest of the state to the Gold Rush. Raiding on both sides went on, but only sporadically and intermittently.[6]

At the time of Kearny and Mason, the basic law governing their relationship with the Indians was the Indian Intercourse Act of 1834.[7] In the whole United States the number of Indian agents allowed under this Act was twelve. The degree of amelioration obtained through the permission to appoint as many sub-agents as the appropriations could afford was lessened through the parsimonious appropriation. Severity of this situation was increased by the annexation of Texas, acquisition of Oregon, and cessions from Mexico of the Southwest.[8]

In 1849 control of the Indians was transferred from the Department of War to the Department of the Interior. John Wilson was appointed Indian Agent at Salt Lake City, "California," on April 7, 1849, to handle the Indians of the west. No doubt there were those naive people at the time who believed some good would derive from the change--none was forthcoming, as history was soon to prove.[9] Transfer of government in California from the military to the civil complicated the action of law and order with respect to both Indian and white population.[10] In the remote mining camps and outlying ranches civil government was carried on through local rules and regulations without authority of the central government. Self-constituted judges dealt roughly with the hapless, and defenseless, Indians. Roving prospectors dealt even more harshly with the individual Indians who came across their paths.[11]

In the north and central areas the Indians were relatively peaceful they lived off the land and out of the rivers. In the south and along the central coastal plain the Mission Indians had been influenced, more or less, by their contact with the Spaniards and Mexicans, and were not troublesome. The trouble-raising, dangerous Indians dwelt in the foothills and in the desert areas. Especially dangerous were the Indian neophytes who had fled from the Missions and joined the bands of "wild" Indians.[12]

Agent of the United States Federal Government promised the Indians of California seven and one-half million acres of land in treaties. The Indians were to give quit-claim deeds for their lands in exchange for the seven and one-half million acres to be maintained as reservations. Also the government promised to provide agricultural implements and other goods, to retain skilled instructors and supervisors in farming, blacksmithing, and wood-working to teach the Indians civilized skills. Complete and immediate compliance was made with the terms of the treaties by the Indians.[13]

Three commissioners had been appointed to negotiate the treaties. In the bill of authorization Congress appropriated only $25,000 to implement the consummation of peaceful settlement of the Indian problem in California. The agents were Redick McKee of Virginia, George W. Barbour of Kentucky, and O. M. Wozencraft of Louisiana. They arrived in California in January of 1851. They found armed companies of trigger-happy whites marching and counter-marching in quasi-military fashion about the Sierra slopes wantonly killing "hostile" Indians.[14]

The commissioners for the Indians were to contact the Indians and make treaties with them that would protect and provide them with the bare necessities of life. Even men armed with many assistants, actual power to usurp and alienate land, and adequate appropriations of monies would have found difficulty in carrying out the assignment that was given to Wozencraft, Barbour, and McKee. These men have been subjected to criticism for their poor judgment and their failure to accomplish the task set for them, but certainly much of the blame lies with the Congress of the United States.

Congress had succumbed to the pressures from interests in California which ran counter to the welfare of the Indians of California.[15]

The three commissioners could have set up any form of division of labor that they wished, but they decided to work in concert for the immediate time after arrival in California. They replaced the form of agency that had been originated under Stephen W. Kearny in 1847. John Augustus Sutter, Mariano Guadalupe Vallejo, and J. D. Hunter had been the associates attempting to find a solution to the Indian problem.[16] When the Department of the Interior was organized in the Government of the United States it sent Adam Johnston as sub-agent for California. Incidental to his investigation of general conditions in California Thomas Butler King, agent of the United States Department of State, reported that it would be better for all concerned if the Indians were concentrated on reservations.[17]

Having rejected the old form of handling the Indian situation, discussed above, the commissioners immediately set out to pacify the Indians. On March 19th six tribes of Indians on the Mariposa River signed away all rights and claims to their property. In exchange for the title to their fertile lands they received some property between the Merced and Tuolumne Rivers and some blankets and beads.

The next month saw a site named Camp Barbour on the upper San Joaquin River established. Camp Barbour was the scene of a tentative treaty on April 14th. On April 19th a formal treaty was arrived at between the commissioners and sixteen tribes, or bands, of roving Indians. In exchange for their lands they were promised a fair sized tract of land somewhere else. Also they were promised food and articles of agricultural use.

The first reservation of the three commissioners had established between the Tuolumne and Merced Rivers was reported to domicile between 600 and 700 Indians. Hopes were high that this number would be increased to 1,000 or 2,000 when the "hostile" Indians were finally rounded up and sold on the idea of giving up their life of happy raiding for one of bovine contentment.

At the second reservation, Camp Barbour on the San Joaquin River, there were about 700 Indians with hopes of an increase to 2,000. With these great victories the three commissioners were sure they had the problem of what to do with the Indians of California solved, or at least well on the road to being solved. In fact they sent a message to the Indian Bureau reporting that the two treaties had broken the confidence of the Indians in their ability to contend with the whites.[18]

The commissioners now tried running the State of California Indian affairs each in a district of his own. The gentleman from Virginia, Redick McKee, became agent of the Northern District which included that portion of the state north of 40° or 41° of latitude, until it reaches the headwaters of the Sacramento River. The gentleman from Louisiana, O.M. Wozencraft, became agent of the Middle District from the Coast Range to the eastern boundary of the state and extending from the southern line of McKee's agency to the northern line of Barbour's district, which was the big bend of the San Joaquin River south and west, and east to the state boundary. On May 13th Barbour met with twelve tribes on the Kings River and successfully negotiated treaties with them. He met with seven tribes on the Kaweah River on May 30th with the same success, and a few days later, June 3rd, he made a treaty with four tribes on Paint Creek. He capped his triumphal journey on June 10th at Tejon Pass with a treaty encompassing the rich lands of eleven bands of unsuspecting aborigines.[19]

In the meantime McKee and Wozencraft obtained treaties, on the 24th to 28th, with six tribes at Dent and Vantine's Ferry on the Stanislaus River, and ten tribes at Camp Union on the Yuba River. On August 1st to 9th nine tribes near Bidwell's Ranch on Chico Creek were inveigled into giving up their patrimony. Five tribes at Reading's Ranch did likewise on August 16th. On September 2nd eight tribes at Camp Colus signed, and on

September 18th four tribes on the Cosumnes River turned their all over to the commissioners. There were twelve miscellaneous tribes near Chico that also signed a treaty with the agent. The prescribed and usual formalities of treaty making in California were closed with two treaties in Southern California. One was signed on January 5, 1852, with three tribes in the Los Angeles area, and the other was signed on January 7, 1852, with the Diegueno Indians. The last of the treaties were received at the Capitol in Washington, D.C. by February 18, 1852,[20] and sponsored unreservedly by both the Commissioner of Indian Affairs, Luke Lea, and the Superintendent of Indian Affairs, Edward F. Beale. The eighteen treaties were tendered to the President of the United States on June 1st. They were considered in secret sessions by Congress and were rejected with a ban of secrecy placed upon them. They were then forgotten by the white man for over fifty years, but the Indians had every word engraved in their minds and lived by the treaties as well as the whites would allow them.[21]

It has been advanced as a reason for the dismissal of the treaties by Congress that the Senate feared the cost. The funds allotted to the three commissioners had been spent and drafts drawn on the Department of the Interior for an additional million dollars. Actually it would seem that the real reason for burying the treaties in Washington was due to the pressure brought to bear by California interests through their Congressmen who held the balance of power in the Congress.

The situation in California was desperate for the Indians and Congress had to do something. On March 1, 1852, an act of Congress created a California Indian Superintendency. The appointment to this office was given to the National Superintendent of Indian Affairs, Edward F. Beale. An appropriation of $100,000 was made for the preservation, protection and regulation of the California Indians. Beale arrived in San Francisco on September 16, 1852, and immediately wrote his plan to his superior, Luke Lea:

In the first place I propose a system of "military posts" to be established on reservations to be regarded as military reservations. The Indians to be invited to assemble within these reserves.

A system of discipline and instruction to be adopted by the agent who is to live at the post.

Each reservation to contain a military establishment. The expense of the troops to be borne by the surplus of Indian labor.

The reservation to be made with a view to a change in location, where increase of white population may make it necessary.[22]

This sounds familiar. The fathers, many years before, set up almost the same type of system under the heading of Missions.

It seems that everyone concerned was willing to try anything that came to mind with regard to the regulation and elimination of the Indian problem. Beale managed to get his appropriation raised to $250,000 and started on the Tejon Reservation experiment. He induced the Indians there to cultivate the land, and it is reported that there was much enthusiasm on his part. In Washington Beale's enemies, jealous of the appropriations, made trouble for him. In the Spring of 1854 the poor bookkeeping of Beale landed him in the middle of a Congressional inquiry as to how the $250,000 appropriation had been spent. After May 1, 1854, the appropriation was cut to $125,000 and Beale was suspended from office pending investigation.[23] The number of reservations authorized was cut from five to three.

On June 2, 1854, the new Superintendent of California Indian Affairs, Thomas J. Henley, was given his commission and instructions. He arrived at the Tejon Reservation on July 15th, but did little to change the order of things as established by Beale. In September he established a reservation at Nome Lackee, in Colusa County. Henley petitioned Congress for permission to establish the originally planned five reservations and for the money appropriation to facilitate their establishment. He asked for $200,000. Imagine how Henley must have felt when the United States Congress appropriated $360,300 for his projected budget, 1855-56.

By September, 1856, Henley was directly instrumental in organizing and establishing reservations at Klamath and Mendocino, and carrying on the Tejon and Nome Lackee projects. Henley also established temporary reserves, or farms, on the Fresno and Kings Rivers, and at Nome Cult Valley in the Coast Range. Henley wrote reports of the progress in eliminating the Indian problem in California by domestication of the Indians. The only drawback was the reports of the United States Army Officers of the detachments at the reservations. They described the laziness, drunkenness and general knavish character of the California Indians. As a result of conflicting reports Congress authorized Godard Bailey to visit the reservations as a special agent. The year 1858 found Bailey making his rounds of the California reservations. Bailey was an honest man and not out to grind any axes. His report was an attack on no one in particular, but he truthfully stated the unhappy failure of Beale's attempt, carried on by Henley, to collect the Indians on self-supporting farms. The immediate result was the cutting of the appropriation in 1859 for the California Indian Superintendency.[24]

Now it was time for Congress to pass another bill; make another stab in the dark at settling the Indian problem of California. It seems that no member of our governing body in Washington ever revived the buried treaties, which had delivered Indian lands to white settlers in exchange for land which, when the Indians arrived on it, had already been sold to other white settlers. This was the process which left the Indians with no land to call their own untill Beale and Henley managed to secure some poor bits of land for farming purposes.

Alfred B. Greenwood, serving under Secretary of the Interior Thompson as Indian Commissioner, felt that the policy that had been followed in California for the handling of the Indians was all wrong. He observed that no right of the Indians with regard to the land was recognized by either the State of California or the United States Federal Government. The farms and reservations were small, widespread, and unsuitable for animal husbandry or agriculture. Greenwood was worried about the speedy extinction of the Indians.

His really unique plan for the handling of the Indians was an abolition of the reservations and farms and the division of the state into two parts. Each district thus created would have a single agent appointed to inform the Indians that they would no longer be fed and clothed at government expense and would have to supply all their own wants by their own efforts.[25] We may well ask how reactionary and to what extent of paradoxical imagery can an official of our government go? In statute following statute, and in law case after law case, the fact that the Indians were not becoming civilized because of their isolated reservations had been decried prior to Greenwood's time. The fact that all of the fertile land was in the hands of white men, and none was available to give away to the Indians never seems to have occurred to Greenwood. He called for the exchange of one form of reservation for another. To take what little food and clothing away from the Indian that the government was giving him and tell him he was on his own on some agriculturally poor land would certainly accelerate the extinction of the Indian, not save the Indian from "the speedy extinction with which he was threatened."

On June 19, 1860, Congress passed the bill dividing California into a Northern and Southern Indian District. Two superintending agents were appointed. The new policy provided for the extension of small reservations over the state. This establishment of large numbers of small reservations over California marks the one contribution to Indian policy in general to come out of California.[26]

The legal status of the Indian improved somewhat under Section 1 of the California Statutes promulgated in 1850 for the protection and government of the Indians. This section provided that all cases involving Indians should come under the jurisdiction of justices of the peace. By the Act of 1856 some authority dealing with corporal punishment of Indians for conviction of theft conferred on justices of the peace was repealed. Justices of the peace lost their authority to try and punish Indians for grand larceny by the Act of April 20, 1863.[27]

An incidental piece of irony can be found in The People v. Juan Antonio, California Reports 27, Tuttle 1864-1865, pp. 404-408. In this case the Supreme Court of California referred to the Act of 1850 as the Act for the Protection and Punishment of the Indians.

FOOTNOTES

[1] Felix S. Cohen, "Original Indian Title," Minnesota Law Review, XXXII (1947-48), 28-59.

[2] Compiled Laws of the State of California, compiled by S. Garfielde, 1853 (Boston: Press of the Franklin Printing House, 1853), pp. 822-825. Sec. 20 of "Law for the Government and Protection of the Indians."

[3] Supra, pp. 11-14.

[4] Compiled Laws of the State of California, op. cit., Sec. 6.

[5] Herbert Howe Bancroft, The History of California (San Francisco: The History Co., 1890).

[6] Edward Everett Dale, The Indians of the Southwest (Norman: The University of Oklahoma Press, 1949), pp. 176-178.

[7] Loc. cit.

[8] Felix S. Cohen, Handbook of Federal Indian Law (Washington, D.C. Government Printing Office, 1942), p. 28.

[9] Dale, loc. cit.

[10] Cohen, "Original Indian Title," op. cit., p. 41.

[11] Chauncey Shafter Goodrich, "The Legal Status of the California Indian," California Law Review, XIV (1926), 89.

[12] Bancroft, loc. cit.

[13] Goodrich, op.cit., pp. 83-100.

[14] George Clark, Indians of Yosemite Valley and Vicinity (Yosemite: George Clark Press, 1907), pp. 1-30.

[15] J. W. Caughey, California (New York: Prentice-Hall, Inc., 1953), p. 325.

[16] Loc. cit.

[17] Dale, op. cit., p. 82.

[18] McKee, Barbour, and Wozencraft to Lea, May 1, 1851, in Senate Executive Documents, 31st Cong., 1st sess., no. 1, p. 486.

[19] Dale, loc. cit.

[20] Goodrich, loc. cit.

[21] Charles C. Royce, Indian Land Cessions in the United States (Washington, D.C.: Smithsonian Institute Reports, 1899).
Alban W. Hoopes, Indian Affairs and Their Administration, with Special Reference to the Far West, 1849-1860 (Philadelphia: 1932).

[22] Beale to Lea, September 16, October 2, 1852, in Senate Executive Documents, 33rd Cong., spec. sess., no. 4, pp. 36, 374.

[23] Subsequent investigations by the Comptroller to the Secretary of the Treasury cleared Beale, April 9, 1885.

[24] William H. Ellison, "The Federal Indian Policy in California, 1846-1860," Mississippi Valley Historical Review, IX (1922), 37-67.

[25] Hoopes, op. cit., p. 112.

[26] (Author did not list.)

[27] Compiled Laws of the State of California, Passed at sessions of 1850-51-52-53, compiled by S. Garfielde (Benecia: Garfielde, 1853).

CHAPTER III

LEGAL STATUS OF THE INDIAN AFTER THE

CIVIL WAR, 1865-1900

After the Civil War the 14th Amendment was added to the Constitution of the United States. This Amendment declares that "all persons born or naturalized in the United States and subject to the jurisdiction thereof, are citizens of the United States and of the state wherein they reside." In spite of the unequivocal language used in the 14th Amendment, Attorney-General Caleb Cushing, in 1855, took a turn around a fantastic course of logic in an attempt to prove that the Indian is not a citizen of the United States within the terms of the 14th Amendment. In his Opinion 750 he readily admits that the Indian is not a foreigner or alien; but they are "domestic subjects." As subjects they are not citizens for the same reason that a slave is not a citizen, is Cushing's reasoning. The Indian is not within the Naturalization Acts which apply to foreigners under other allegiance; and neither are the Indians capable of citizenship because of place or time of birth, "an incapacity of his race."[1] Daniel Webster declaimed in Johnson v. McIntosh[2] that the Indians "are of that class who are said by the jurists not to be citizens, but perpetual inhabitants with diminutive rights."[3]

As one looks through the records to discover some status for the Indian it appears that there is not a question but that

> . . . independently of the constitutional provision it has always been the doctrine of this country, except as applied to Africans brought here and sold as slaves, that birth within the dominion and jurisdiction of the United States itself creates citizenship.[4] [Except in the case of the American Indian.]

In McKay v. Campbell it was held that "to be a citizen of the United States by reason of his birth, a person must not only be born within its territorial limits, but also he must be born subject to its jurisdiction--that is, in its power and obedience." Each time we read such statements by the learned court there always follows another statement that runs somewhat in this vein: "The plaintiff is a citizen of the United States if no other factor but his place of birth, and time of birth, were in question; but, unless being an Indian puts him in another class of people who do not live under the jurisdiction of the United States." Then, by devious methods, it can be shown somehow that the Indian under question is in another class. In the Matter of Heff the question is pointedly asked whether the Indian is to be considered of a special class forever.[5] The swing back and forth in our courts was reflected in a decision statement like the following:

> . . . we think it too firmly and clearly established to admit of dispute, that the Indian tribes residing within the territorial limits of the United States are subject to their authority, and where the country occupied by them is not within the limits of one of the states, Congress may by law punish any offense committed there, no matter whether the offender be a white man or an Indian.[6]

The United States Supreme Court, in United States v. Rogers, admitted the power the Congress had to punish offenders in the territorial limits of the United States, whether they be white or red, as early as 1846. In cases appearing before the United States Supreme Court as late as 1911 the point was held that Congress had the power over all territory within the boundaries of the United States. Congress had given powers to superintendents, agents, and sub-agents who have been called czaristic in their overwhelming scope.[7]

Could the government give and take away rights and privileges from the Indians at the whim of government? Did not the individual Indian have any right to say what he did or did not want done with his person? Was there no degree of self-determination and consent for the Indian? In some places the government assumed guardianship of the Indians, and then abandoned it by making a pretense of giving citizenship, and then at a later time resuming the guardianship status.

The courts have made answer, in effect: the various courts have been of the opinion that the government had the right to place the Indian under the police powers of the Congress and remove them at its discretion. This removal once taken place could not be reinstituted without the consent of the individual Indians and the state in which they resided. Then doctrine was laid down controlling the Indian as a ward.

1. Incompetent persons, though citizens, may not have the full right to control their persons and property.

2. The mere fact that citizenship has been conferred upon Indians does not necessarily end the right or duty of the United States to pass laws in their interest as a dependent people.

3. Citizenship is not in itself an obstacle to the exercise by Congress of its power to enact laws for the benefit and protection of tribal Indians as a dependent people.

4. The guardianship of the United States continues, notwithstanding the citizenship conferred upon the allottees.

5. The guardianship arises from their condition of tutelage or dependency; and it rests with Congress to determine when the relationship shall cease; the mere grant of rights of citizenship not being sufficient to terminate it. [8]

With regard to these doctrines it is interesting to note, just incidentally, that in the case of Rancisco v. the IAC the point was finally made in 1923 that an Indian shall not be classified as incompetent merely because he is an Indian. It was proven to the satisfaction of the court that Francisco, an Indian, was more capable of pursuit of his particular job than anyone else in his county. [9] As protector of the individual Indian it has been found and held by the courts that the United States is duty bound to protect the individual Indian even after he has become a citizen of one of the several states. [10]

In view of later events it is almost unbelievable that in the first instance the Indian Agent of the United States Government went to the Indian as the ambassador to the court of a foreign nation. The Indian Agents who were conscientious men outnumbered the unscrupulous ones, and with time many Indian groups entrusted their very existence to these men. In cases of this nature the Indian Agent was compelled to assume unauthorized power. The troubles of the Indians, many times, developed after the self-sacrificing and honorable agent who had won their trust was removed. Even where civil and military agents with the welfare of the Indian at heart struggled, where loyal teachers and consecrated missionaries labored, the lack of law made any gains negligible. The United States Government's treatment of the Indian has been said to be the culmination of inconsistency, injustice, and folly. They have been herded like cattle, and shut off from contact with civilization.

Sir William Blackstone, the eminent British jurist, wrote of basic rights that the most important right of justice was ability to apply to the courts for redress of injuries. Sir Edward Coke, second only to Sir William Blackstone in jurisprudence, nails down the right of justice more firmly when he wrote: "Therefore every man shall have justice and right for the injury done to him, freely without sale, fully without any denial, and speedily without delay."[11] It is a travesty on our ideals of democracy and equality that the Indians in our midst have been denied the very basic rights that Sir William Blackstone and Sir Edward Coke wrote about.

A review of the rights of the Indians until well into this century reveals evidence that the only right given to them was the right to do away with themselves. The fact that the Indians in the several states had little or no rights because of the lack of interest in them was decried by the Honorable Hubert Work, Secretary of the Interior in 1925. The reason he gave for this was that the Indians paid no state taxes and were not permitted to vote. Either by law or by custom the Indian has been deprived of any legal right to elect representatives and pay property taxes in the several states. New Mexico passed laws as early as 1854 in which even the comparatively highly cultured Pueblo Indians were excluded from the privilege of voting at the popular elections of the territory.[12] Education, medicine, housing, rehabilitation, and the other assets of progress that made the white man's standard of living in the United States so high are often passed on to the Indians living in our midst. That this is being remedied by our legislative bodies is to be applauded. In the past our courts have stated that the Indian could in no capacity claim redress in our courts. The legal right of the Indian is sanctimoniously declared; but the legal remedy before the law is denied him. It was the opinion of the Attorney General that their rights were recognized, but not enforced.[13]

In spite of the overwhelming evidence to the contrary, the United States Government has made valiant attempts to do the basically right thing by the Indians in so far as was possible. Thomas Jefferson commented:

> . . . that the lands of this country were taken from them [the Indians] by conquest, is not so general a truth as is supposed. I find in our historians and records, repeated proofs of purchase, which cover a considerable part of the lower country; and many more would doubtless be found on further search. The upper country, we know, has been acquired altogether by purchases made in the most unexceptional form.[14]

Jefferson was commenting on the general misconception held that the United States either acquired this country by conquest or by purchase from some European country; France, Britain, or Spain. It is true that we paid approximately fifty million dollars to the above mentioned countries for the right of government and sovereignty. The land purchased for fifteen million dollars from Napoleon was owned by Spanish, French and American settlers. That part of the Louisiana Purchase not owned by white men was owned by the Indians dwelling thereon. Napoleon had his money for the land, but the United States paid over 300 million dollars more to Indians in this territory for their

land. The Indians still kept out enough land for themselves that the current
annual income is more than the original purchase price to Napoleon. Two
articles of the treaty which transferred Louisiana from France to the United
States are of interest to the student of Indian rights. It was provided:

> Article III. The inhabitants of the ceded territory shall be incor-
> porated in the Union of the United States, and admitted as soon as
> possible, according to the principles of the federal constitution, to
> the principles of the federal constitution, to the enjoyment of all
> the rights, advantages and immunities of citizens of the United States;
> and in the meantime they shall be maintained and protected in the
> free enjoyment of their liberty, property, and the religion they pro-
> fess.

> Article IV. The United States promise to execute such treaties
> and articles as may have been agreed between Spain and the tribes
> and nations of Indians, until by mutual consent of the United States
> and the said tribes or nations, other suitable articles shall have
> been agreed upon. [15]

In spite of the fact that much was promised we have seen that Indians
in many places, California included, did not receive the money, goods, ser-
vices, and lands which they had been promised. [16] Congress has allowed the
Indians to sue the United States in the Court of Claims for compensation that
was promised under the pigeon-holed treaties made in California during the
1850's. The Court of Claims found that the Indians should have seventeen
million dollars owing them. By the time the government got through with the
deductions the amount was a trifle over five million dollars. [17]

Indian property rights have been recognized by the United States
Government to a greater extent than the rights of the aborigines of South
America, Australia and Canada have been recognized by the white men who
have settled on their lands. After other lands had been discovered and declared for the monarchs of the respective country the monarchs in turn handed
the land and inhabitants over to sycophants, and the like, who never visited or
developed the land thus acquired. In the part of North America encompassed

by the United States the monies expended by the federal treasury were replaced to a certain extent by the sale of the land purchased from the Indians
to individual settlers who proved up the land and had a very personal interest in its development. The wonder of the whole westward expansion to the
Pacific Ocean is not at what inequities there were, but that in the negotia-
tions for these millions of square miles of land there was not more inequity
and bloodshed.

In the past several forms of action were used to obtain land from
the Indians. Some of the land was taken through treaty, some through use
of the United States Army, and some through other legal forms. As long as
the Indians were able to play the United States off against England, France
or Spain they were treated in their several tribes as sovereign. After the
cession of Louisiana by France, in 1803, and our stalemate in the war with
Britain in 1814, and obtaining Florida from Spain in 1819, the treatment of
the Indians as sovereign entities began to decline. It was of the period following that general crook wrote, ". . . the Indian commands respect for his
rights only so long as he inspires terror for his rifle." This was well for
the Indian until he was overborne by sheer weight of numbers by the white
man and the white man's superior tactics and fire power. The outrages re-
portedly perpetrated by the Indians were acts of revenge that mirrored the
denial of protection under law and a legal, peaceful means of settlement of
grievances.[18] The military was used for the restraint and domination of the
Indians from shortly after the Revolutionary War into the late 1890's. No
one has ever claimed to organize all of the facts and figures pertaining to
the cost in time, money, and lives the settling of the West cost for this cruel
and unenlightened way of operating. In 1870 it was officially estimated that
the Indian wars had cost the government in excess of one million dollars for
every dead Indian.

Commissioner Taylor asked a question in 1868: "Shall our Indians
be civilized, and how?" He then answered the question he had asked.

Assuming that the government has a right, and that it is its duty to solve the Indian question definitely and decisively, it becomes necessary that it determine at once the best and speediest method of its solution, and then, armed with right, to act in the interest of both races.

If might makes right, we are the strong and they the weak; and we would do no wrong to proceed by the cheapest and nearest route to the desired end, and could, therefore, justify ourselves in ignoring the natural as well as the conventional rights of the Indians, if they stand in the way, and, as their lawful masters, assign them their status and their tasks, or put them out of their own way and our by extermination with the sword, starvation, or by any other method.

If, however, they have rights as well as we, then clearly it is our duty as well as sound policy to so solve the question of their future relations to us and each other, as to secure their rights and promote their highest interest, in the simplest, easiest, and most economical way possible.

But to assume they have no rights is to deny the fundamental principles of Christianity, as well as to contradict the whole theory upon which the government has uniformly acted towards them; we are therefore bound to respect their rights, and, if possible, make our interests harmonize with them.[19]

The question was answered quite differently by subsequent Indian Commissioners. Commissioner Walker held sway in 1872, and he had a lot to say, fortunately much of it was put in writing and we can read the feelings of a certain portion of our officials with regard to the Indians. On the following pages the writer will quote extensively from Commissioner Walker because it is evident that the way he felt was mirrored in the feelings of men in Washington and in the field. In the 1872 Report of the Commission on Indian Affairs, Walker wrote in defense of the government's policy of appeasing the Indians as follows:

The Indian policy, so called, of the Government, is a policy, and it is not a policy, or rather it consists of two policies, entirely distinct, seeming, indeed to be mutually inconsistent and to reflect each upon the other; the one regulating the treatment of the tribes which are potentially hostile, that is, whose hostility is only repressed just so long as, and so far as, they are supported in idleness by the Government; the other regulating the treatment of those tribes which, from traditional friendship, from numerical weakness, or by the force of their location, are either indisposed toward, or incapable of, resistance to the demands of the Government.

It is, of course, hopelessly illogical that the expenditures of the Government should be proportioned not to the good but to the ill desert of the several tribes; that large bodies of Indians should be supported in entire indolence by the bounty of the Government simply because they are audacious and insolent, while well-disposed Indians are only assisted to self-maintenance, since it is known they will not fight.

. . . and yet, after all this, the Government is right and its critics wrong; and the Indian Policy is sound, sensible, and beneficent, because it reduces to the minimum the loss of life and property along our frontier, and allows the freest development of our settlements and railways possible under the circumstances.

There is no question of national dignity, be it remembered, involved in the treatment of savages by a civilized power. With wild men, as with wild beasts, the question whether in a given situation one shall fight, coax, or run, is a question merely of what is easiest and safest.

The writer does not believe the paragraphs just quoted show a healthy attitude toward the problem of governing subject peoples within the boundaries of a powerful nation. This is not all that comes to light in reading the pages of the Reports of the Indian Affairs Commission for 1872. Commissioner Walker believed that the Indian Reservation should exist for the following purposes:

. . . the Indians should be made as comfortable on, and as uncomfortable off, their reservations as it was in the power of the Government to make them; that such of them as went right should be protected and fed, and such as went wrong should be harassed and scourged without intermission . . . . Such a use of the strong arm of the Government is not war, but discipline. . . The reservation system affords the place for thus dealing with tribes and bands, without the access of influences inimical to peace and virtue. It is only necessary that Federal laws, judiciously framed to meet all the facts of the case, and enacted in season, before the Indians begin to scatter, shall place all the members of this race under a strict reformatory control by the agents of the Government. Especially is it essential that the right of the Government to keep Indians upon the reservations assigned to them, and to arrest and return them whenever they wander away, should be placed beyond dispute.

It belongs not to a sanguine, but to a sober view of the situation, that three years will see the alternative of war eliminated from the

Indian question, and the most powerful and hostile bands of today thrown in entire helplessness on the mercy of the Government . . . No one certainly will rejoice more heartily than the present Commissioner when the Indians of this country cease to be in a position to dictate, in any form or degree, to the Government; when, in fact, the last hostile tribe becomes reduced to the condition of suppliants for charity.

This was written a year before the Modoc uprising in California and four years before the Battle of the Little Big Horn in which the alleged hero of many an Indian battle was killed with his entire command. And it was many more than three years after 1872 before the alternative of war with the Indians was eliminated.

There is little wonder that such atrocities were perpetrated on the Indians in the field when the orders were given by men reflecting the limited vision of their time. The placing of the Modoc Indians on a Klamath Reservation where the Modocs could not possibly stay because of their age-old enmity with the Klamaths; the driving into Indian Territory of the Northern Cheyennes; the destruction of the orchards and crops of the Navahos with the subsequent removal of the whole tribe to Fort Union in the New Mexico Territory; all reflect the attitude of the officials of the United States Government following the Civil War. At random the writer will recount what happened when the policies of the United States Government were put into a little more solid form than sanguinary words. When the form was steel and lead in the western plains and hills it sounded differently from mere words.

In 1877 the last of the bands of the Northern Cheyennes, under their chief, Dull Knife, were forced to surrender. The band was moved south to Indian Territory. Used to the rolling hills with grass and forests, streams and lakes, the barren wilderness with change of climate caused much sickness and death in the band. In September, 1878, Dull Knife and Little Wolf ceased their requests for removal back to the north country and led 320 of the band toward freedom. In a very short time the escaping band was overtaken by the United States Army. During a parley which followed the overtaking, Little Wolf declared that the Indians did not want to fight because there was no chance of victory for the Indians, but they would not return to the reservation from which they had just fled. The troops immediately fired into the band of almost unarmed Indians. Some authors write of this incident as a mistake, but this same scene had been, and has been, recreated so many times in America that we may as well call it only an incident. The battle was short and the forty-nine men, fifty-one women, and forty-eight children who survived the massacre were carried as prisoners to Fort Robinson. Even locked in an open corral of the fort in Nebraska in January with temperatures reaching 40° below zero, the Indians refused to return to Indian Territory reservations from which they had fled. Orders from the Department of the Interior to the commandant at Fort Robinson pre-emptorily directed the removal of the Cheyennes to the reservation. The acting spokesman for the tribe, Wild Hog, made answer that they would die, but would not return to the reservation. Then the Army kept the Indians for five days and nights with no food or fuel, and for the last three days without water. The Indians broke out of their place of confinement and fled into a blinding snow storm. This was undoubtedly what the commanding officer was waiting for. The Army rode off and cut out the stragglers until finally, twelve days after the break, the remnants of the Indian band was driven into a ravine some fifty miles from Fort Robinson. Of the one hundred and forty-eight originally brought to the fort, many were killed by starvation and exposure before the break and many others were killed in the chase and storm. In the ravine were twenty-four Indians with only a few guns, very little ammunition, and a few hunting knives. The troopers surrounded the ravine and closed in. After the single volley of ammunition was exhausted by the Indians (killing a lieutenant and two privates) they rushed the troops with their knives, a pace or two and they were cut down. The bodies of Indians numbered seventeen male, five female, and two children. One wounded Indian and eight women, five of them wounded, were returned to the fort from which they had fled. Of the 320 Cheyennes who had fled from the reservation the previous September only seven wounded were sent back.[20]

In all fairness to the administration of the judiciary the writer feels he must include the account that is somewhat parallel to the terrible details just reviewed. A band of Ponca Indians had been taken to Indian Territory and placed on a reservation. The band, led by their chief, Standing Bear, fled into Nebraska and took up abode with the Omaha Indian Tribe. Many of the Poncas had intermarried with the Omahas and there had been a friendly feeling between the groups for a long time. Their language and living habits were the same. The Poncas were accepted into the group and given jobs and share-crop farms. The Ponca Indians gave up their tribal identity and disbanded as an organization and did all in their power to cut loose from the United States Government.

The United States Army appeared on the Omaha lands and sought to arrest Chief Standing Bear and the Poncas and return them to Indian Territory where 158 of the tribe had died of disease out of the original number of 581 who had been herded by the army from the Dakotas to the Territory the year previous. Brigadier General George Crook, Commander of the Military Department of the Platte, was ordered to remove the Poncas. Attorneys retained by Standing Bear sued out a writ of <u>habeas corpus</u>[21] against General Crook. The ground was that Standing Bear and his band had renounced their membership in the Ponca Tribe. Since they were no longer Ponca Indians no power could force them to live on the Ponca Reservation. Judge Dundy stated in his sustaining decision:

> They claim to be unable to see the justice, or reason, or wisdom, or necessity, of removing them by force from their own native plains and blood relations to a far-off country, in which they can see little but new-made graves opening for their reception. The land from which they fled in fear has no attractions for them. The love of home and native land was strong enough in the minds of these people to induce them to brave every peril to return and live and die where they

had been reared . . . .

In view of the foregoing facts the court reached the conclusion that the Indian relators . . . did all they could to separate themselves from their tribe and to sever their tribal relations, for the purpose of becoming self-sustaining and living without support from the government. This being so, it presents the question as to whether or not an Indian can withdraw from his tribe, sever his tribal relation therewith, and terminate his allegiance thereto, for the purpose of making an independent living and adopting our own civilization . . . .

I think the individual Indian possesses the clear and God-given right to withdraw from his tribe and forever live away from it, as though it had no further existence. If the right of expatriation was open to doubt in this country down to the year 1868, certainly since that time no sort of question as to the right can now exist. On the 27th of July of that year Congress passed an act, now appearing as section 1999 of the revised statutes, which declares that: "Whereas, the right of expatriation is a natural and inherent right of all people, indispensable to the enjoyment of the rights of life, liberty, and the pursuit of happiness; and, whereas, in the recognition of this principle the government has freely received emigrants from all nations, and invested them with the rights of citizenship . . . . Therefore, any declaration, instruction, opinion, order, or decision of any officer of the United States which denies, restricts, impairs, or questions the right of expatriation, is declared inconsistent with the fundamental principles of the republic. [22]

In 1876 Commissioner John Q. Smith answered the question asked in 1868 by Commissioner Taylor in a different way from that in which Commissioner Walker had. The answer is in the form of an apology.

. . . No new hunting-grounds remain, and the civilization or the utter destruction of the Indians is inevitable. The next twenty-five years are to determine the fate of a race. If they cannot be taught, and taught very soon, to accept the necessities of their situation and begin in earnest to provide for their own wants by labor in civilized pursuits, they are destined to speedy extinction. [23]

Whereas there have been cases in which the Indians in other portions of the United States have been allowed to win their cases this has not been true in California until very recent times. In spite of the fact that no disability was placed upon the Indians of California at the State Constitutional Convention there was no implementation placed on the record enfranchising them. By ignoring the Indian problem the post-Civil War citizens of California placed their Indian neighbors well on the road to extinction.

FOOTNOTES

[1] Henry Spaciman Pancost, The Indian before the Law (Philadelphia: Printed by order of the executive committee of the Indian Rights Association, 1884), p. 31.

[2] Johnson v. McIntosh, 8 Wheaton 574.

[3] Pancost, op. cit., pp. 31-33.

[4] In re Look Tin Sing, 21 Fed. 905, 909; McKay v. Campbell, 2 Sawyer 118, 122.

[5] Chauncy Shafter Goodrich, "The Legal Status of the California Indian," California Law Review, XIV (1926).

[6] United States v. Rogers, 4 How. 567 (1846).

[7] Hallowell v. United States, 221 U.S. 317 (1911); also in United States v. Kagama, 118 U.S. 375 (1886); Willoughby, The Constitution of the United States (1929), p. 439.

[8] In Matter of Heff, 197 U.S. 488, 508-9.

[9] Francisco v. Industrial Accident Commission, 192 Cal. 635.

[10] Cramer v. U.S., 43 S. Ct. 342, 261 U.S. 219.

[11] Pancost, op. cit., p. 33.

[12] Laws, 1854-55, p. 142, #3: Comp. Laws 1897, #1678.

[13] Opinion Attorney-General, p. 466 (Wm. Wirt).

[14] From Notes on the State of Virginia, 1781-85, reprinted in Padover, "The Complete Jefferson," (1943), p. 632. (Minnesota Law Review, XXXII [1947].

[15] Treaty of April 30, 1803, United States and France for the cession of the Territory of Louisiana.

[16] Felix S. Cohen, "Original Indian Title," Minnesota Law Review, XXXII (1948), 34-36.

[17] Ibid., p. 38.

[18] Pancost, op. cit., p. 36.

[19] Report of the Commission on Indian Affairs, 1868, p. 16.

[20] Described in Conners v. United States et al., 33 C. Cls., 317 (1898).

[21] Habeas corpus ad subjiciendum. Person deprived of liberty submits to and agrees to receive whatever the judge or court shall think fit.

[22] U.S. ex rel. Standing Bear v. Crook, (C.C. Neb. 1879) 5 Dill. 453, 25 Fed. Cas. No. 14,891. See also Walter Hart Blumenthal, American Indians Dispossessed (Philadelphia: Geo. S. MacManus Co., 1955), p. 186.

[23] Report of the Commission on Indian Affairs, 1876, p. 6.

CHAPTER IV

LEGAL STATUS OF THE INDIAN UNDER

TREATY ARRANGEMENTS

Generally speaking the ideology behind treaties with the aborigines of the newly found lands was based upon the assumption that the invading government had a sovereign authority to match the sovereign authority of the government of the aborigines who held the land. It had to be further assumed that the aborigines as a tribe, clan, or group had a transferable title. Very early it was agreed upon that the government, British, French, Spanish, or United States, should treat with the aborigine in contra-distinction to the individual trapper or settler dealing with him.

The Dutch had the idea that the Indian's right to his land was inviolable. There were some Britons who felt this way also. Our own government from its very inception pledged itself to the protection of, and friendship with, the various tribes and groups of Indians. Congress appointed commissioners as early as 1784 to negotiate with the Indians to set boundary lines.

Early in our treating with the Indians it was held that the Indian tribes were of the same degree of sovereignty as any of the other nations in the world with which we had treaties. The same force and dignity was ascribed to them. Even after the Indian Appropriation Act of 1871, which called a halt to the making of treaties with the Indians, there were articles calling for the fulfillment of the treaties which had been made prior to that date. In 1828 Attorney General William Wirt gave his opinion regarding the force of treaties between the United States and Indian tribes. There seemed to be little doubt in his mind but that the Indian was a self-directed, independent individual. The Indians were organized in independent nations which had all the rights of other independent nations to make war and peace, and were governed by laws made by their own councils. Attorney-General Wirt was also of the opinion that the Indian nation which dwelt on the land had title to that land and could dispose of it as the nation saw fit. He summed up his opinion with the logic that if the Indian nation was self-directing and independent and could choose or refuse to treat with the spokesmen of the advancing tide of civilization, with intent to fulfill their part of the contract, they were entitled to hold those with whom they treated and contracted equally bound to the treaties.[1]

Commissioner Parker rings in a Biblical atmosphere in his concept of treating with the Indians. He states all the facts that he sees in the situation and adds platitudes. He felt that in order for a nation to have treaty rights with other nations it must have the military or economic power to force compliance with the compacts made. The stipulations made in a treaty must be of such a nature that both parties to the agreement can fulfill their parts of the agreement. It was Commissioner Parker's opinion that the Indian nations were not sovereign nations with the power to carry out provisions of the treaties the United States had been making with them. He points out the flimsy nature of the possessory rights to the land the Indians held under wardship status. The concept of Indian national entity was fostered in the treaties which had been made generally for the extinguishment of supposed absolute title to the land upon which they roamed. This was a cruel farce to play upon unsuspecting aborigines. In Parker's opinion the "poor Indian has been greatly wronged and ill treated; that this whole country was once his, of which he has been despoiled, and that he has been driven from place to place until he has hardly left to him a spot where to lay his head."[2] He called for legislation in the acquisition of agricultural land needed for the advancing civilization. This legislation should be as liberal and humane as possible for a Christian country to enact.

After the making of treaties with the Indians was abandoned in 1871 Commissioner Edward P. Smith wrote of the inequities arising from the United States Government honoring the treaties made in the past. A double condition of sovereignty and wardship existed side by side. The United States Government made treaties as with sovereign states, and then sent agents to control and supervise the Indians as wards. This dual position resulted immediately in the loss of authority by the chieftain. The loss of internal control of their own destinies brought on a greater dependence upon the bounties of the Government. Commissioner Smith wrote: "So far, and as rapidly as possible, all recognition of Indians in any other relation than strictly as subjects of the government should cease. To provide for this, radical legislation will be required."[3]

To bring the treaty matter down to a later date and observe what the Supreme Court of the United States considers in its decisions where treaties between the United States Government and Indian tribes are on the docket is most succinctly brought out in the case of Jones v. Meehan:[4]

> In construing any treaty between the United States and an Indian tribe, it must always (as was pointed out by the counsel for the appellees) be borne in mind that the negotiations for the treaty are conducted, on the part of the United States, an enlightened and powerful nation, by representatives skilled in diplomacy, masters of a written language, understanding the modes and forms of creating the various technical estates known to their law, and assisted by an interpreter employed by themselves; that the treaty is drawn up by them and in their own language; that the Indians, on the other hand, are a weak and dependent people, who have no written language and are wholly unfamiliar with all the forms of legal expression, and whose only knowledge of the terms in which the treaty is framed is that imparted to them by the interpreter employed by the United States; and that the treaty must therefore be construed, not according to the technical meaning of its words to learned lawyers, but in the sense in which they would naturally be understood by the Indians.

Ambiguities are resolved in favor of the Indians.[5]

The outcome of the act in 1871 that changed the policy of the government in the making of treaties with Indians was that laws could be passed regarding the natives without consulting the Indians. Undoubtedly the real reason for the change in policy was to allow the House of Representatives a chance to have its say in the making of agreements with and for the Indians. In the making of treaties only the Senate had to ratify. The House of Representatives had voted for the appropriations of money to put the treaties into effect and carry them out, but had had no voice in the negotiation of the treaties.

There have been cases where treaties with the Indians have been broken for the benefit of the Indians. Even though the courts tend to hold for the Indians in a treaty violation, if the case ever comes to court there is still no real protection for the Indian in a treaty. For enforcement of a treaty between sovereign nations only the standing armies or economic sanctions of the countries involved can be counted on to force respect of the treaties. There is no liability in the breaking of an Indian treaty, whereas, in the breaking of a treaty with a strong state international law places a liability on the breaker of the treaty.[6]

In the final analysis the courts have at times raised no judicial question to the breaking or abrogation of treaties with the Indians. The courts have stated that the will of Congress over the Indians is supreme.[7]

FOOTNOTES

[1] Opinion Attorney General 110 (1828), Attorney General Wm. Wirt. 16 J. Comp. Leg. 78, 80-81.

[2] Report of the Committee on Indian Affairs, 1869, p. 6.

[3] Report of the Committee on Indian Affairs, 1873, p. 3.

[4] 175 U.S. 1 (1899).

[5] Loc. cit.

[6] Felix S. Cohen, "Indian Rights and the Federal Courts," Minnesota Law Review, XXXII (1947-48), 145-200.

[7] See Leavenworth, et al. Railroad Co. v. U.S. (1876) 92 U.S. 733, 23 L. Ed. 634; Ex Parte Crow Dog, (1883) 109 U.S. 556, 3 Sup. Ct. 396, 27 L. Ed. 1030; U.S. v. Celestine (1909) 215 U.S. 278, 30 Sup. Ct. 93, 54 L. Ed. 195; Thomas v. Gay (1896), 169 U.S. 264, 18 Sup. Ct. 340, 42 L. Ed. 740.

CHAPTER V

LEGAL STATUS OF THE INDIAN UNDER

WARDSHIP ARRANGEMENTS

Definitively the dictionary states that a ward is a person, especially a minor, who has been legally placed under the care of a guardian or a court. It is a state of being under the care or control of a legal guardian. Wardship is guardianship over a minor or some other person legally incapable of managing his own affairs. It is the state of being under restraining guard or in custody. A ward is someone who is under the protection or control of another. In common law the guardian

(a) has custody of the ward's person and can decide where the ward is to reside,

(b) is required to educate and maintain the ward, out of the ward's estate,

(c) is authorized to manage the ward's property, for the benefit of the ward,

(d) is precluded from profiting at the expense of the ward's estate, or acquiring any interest therein,

(e) is responsible to the courts and to the ward, at such time as the ward may become able to act in his own right, for an accounting with respect to the conduct of the guardianship.[1]

The rules laid down under common law show evidence that a state of wardship does not exist between the United States and the Indians residing in the country. In the first usage of the term by Chief Justice John Marshall[2] wardship was used to distinguish relationships between the United States Government and tribes as against between the United States Government and individual Indians. It was not stated by the Chief Justice as a binding, absolute representation of relationship, but only as a likeness of the relationship. It was a device to distinguish the Indian tribe from a national state beyond our territorial limits. Several cases have pointed out that the Spanish and French treated with the Indians in the full knowledge that they were not capable of treating in full equality and needed protection.

Under the common law the guardian has custody of the ward's person and can decide where the ward is to reside. The excuse of wardship is merely a mask for doing things that would not be allowed under the law to other than Indians. Their property is held in trust, and frequently it has been confiscated outright. Through wardship the federal government has taken over offices that would normally have been administered by the states in which the Indians lived.

Wardship has been the excuse under which the government has taken into custody the tribes, which are made up of individuals, so that the logical end in court rulings finally evolved to a far distant point from where they began with Chief Justice Marshall in 1831.[3] The general concept today amongst the people in and out of government is that the individual Indian is a ward of the federal government. The courts have said that state control is replaced in authority by the federal government because of the wardship held over the Indians by the government. It is then a device to incarcerate in concentration camps, on the sides of barren hills, individuals and groups of individuals who are theoretically born free and equal in the United States. There were very few treaties made between the United States and the several Indian tribes that did not call for schools and teachers to be placed on the reservations in proportion to the number of Indians on the reservation. There were very few instances in which this clause of treaties, or facet of wardship responsibility, was ever consummated.[4]

In theory the federal government, as guardian, should be managing the ward's property for the benefit of the ward. Extension of the theory that the government is holding lands for Indians in wardship makes subject lands inalienable. Indians who have fee simple title to their land hold the land without the ability to sell. Property is being held in trust by the government then for men and women who are perfectly capable of taking care of their own affairs. There have been cases where an Indian with fee simple title to property has been released from his status as ward and could alienate his land, and then at a later time had the rights of alienation taken from him. [5] It has been most difficult to get Congress or a court in the past to allow the Indians the equal freedom before the law that a white man enjoys. The Indian was not able to act in his own right, and no accounting has ever been called for with respect to the conduct of the guardian until very recent years.

As wards the Indians have been subject to the most humiliating position of being discriminated against by the Congress of the United States. Many statutes of the federal government are applicable only to the Indian. [6] This is the worst kind of discrimination when laws are passed against a group or individuals, either because of the identification of race, creed, or color. Libraries have been filled on the discrimination against peoples of other races, colors, and creeds; but very little has been written or said about the discrimination against the Indian. [7]

In lieu of the fact that there was never enacted a statute legalizing the concentrating of Indians on reservations, the United States Government used the concept of the ward Indian to vindicate its action in imprisoning the Indians on reservations. By a series of assumed premises, the principal one being that the Indian could not possibly be a citizen of the United States, [8] the government and courts deprived the Indian on the reservation the right of even leaving the reservation without permission.

This is a good place to interpose a rather dreadful picture of what the development of the wardship proposition brings in its wake. Entwined inextricably with wardship is the reservation which has introduced a legion of evils. The abrogation of freedom of worship is the spectre that appears out of the control of the daily lives of the Indians on the reservation. The Methodists, Presbyterians, Roman Catholics, Baptists, and Quakers abhorred the uncivilized and pagan forms of worship that the savages practiced. Under especial attack are the dances labelled cruel, licentious, and demoralizing. As late as 1921 the Office of Indian Affairs reminded reservation officials:

> The sun-dance, and all other similar dances and so-called religious ceremonies are considered "Indian Offences" under existing regulations, and corrective penalties are provided. I regard such restriction as applicable to any [religious] dance which involves . . . the reckless giving away of property . . . frequent or prolonged periods of celebration . . . in fact any disorderly or plainly excessive performance that promotes superstitions, cruelty, licentiousness, idleness, danger to health, and shiftless indifference to family welfare. . . . The Indian dances be limited to one in each month in the daylight hours of one day in the midweek, and at one center in each district; the months of March and April, June, July, and August being excepted. None take part in the dances or be present who are under 50 years of age. A careful propaganda be undertaken to educate public opinion against the dance.[9]

The most deplorable situation which arose out of this kind of restrictive control was the loss over a half a century of many individual tribal cultures. The dances and ceremonies which went to make up, not only the religion, but also the very way of life for the Indian, were lost. Fortunately, the area was too great, geographically, and the number of officers too few to enforce the regulations against the Sun Dance and other basic ceremonies. Much is now being done to revive the culture and religion of the Indians.

Along with the restrictions was the forceful taking of the children from their homes and locking them away in bleak, prison-like boarding schools. Many times the schools were in another state. In these schools many practices were employed to break the spirit of the youth. Mixed dancing lessons were employed with first cousins forced to dance together against all clan and tribal taboos. Many of the schools into which the youth were placed were operated by the religious groups mentioned above. The children were forced to pay lip service to the "Christian" sect into which they were delivered. The boys were not allowed to return home for their coming of age ceremonies, and their hair was forcibly cut short.

It was during President U.S. Grant's administration that Christian missionaries were placed in administrative charge of many Indian reservations. By the very fact of this action the official government sanction was placed upon the concept of no religious freedom of thought for the Indian. Under the rule of the military, then the Interior Department's corrupt agency system, and finally the mission bodies attempt to stamp out Indian culture, it is very nearly a miracle that there is any internal organization or culture left to fan into a flame now. In time of persecution culture traits are frequently given strength rather than being obliterated.

After treaties, statutes, and laws approached the 4,000 plus number; and after every form of suppression known to "civilized" man had been used to crush the Indian, still the spirit of the Indian held. In the face of this inability to crush the Indian, the policy of government changed. In 1928 Secretary of the Interior Work reviewed the failure of the government. He stated that the fixing of separate laws and customs for each group had wrought hardship on the part of the Indians and the whites attempting such administration. There are differences in the several Indian groups in our country, and where treaties and laws affect these differences they are still valid. Secretary Work found that he had inherited a concept from past administrations which had lumped the Indians of America into a general group on the pretext of administrative efficiency and economy. Some of the thought behind this was that the Indians had actually been molded into a single form and all should be treated alike. But the Indian was finding he had champions in both races who were becoming more and more interested in his welfare and civil rights.

On February 1, 1928, the Senate authorized the Committee on Indian

Affairs to survey the conditions related to the Indian of the United States. The resolution that officially launched the first of the great Indian reform movements in our government was worded as follows:

Whereas there are 225,000 Indians presently under the control of the Bureau of Indian Affairs, who are, in contemplation of law, citizens of the United States but who are in fact treated as wards of the Government and are prevented from the enjoyment of the free and independent use of property and of liberty of contract with respect thereto: and

Whereas the Bureau of Indian Affairs handles, leases, and sells Indian property of great value, and disposes of funds which amount to many millions of dollars annually without responsibility to civil courts and without effective responsibility to Congress: and

Whereas it is claimed that the control by the Bureau of Indian Affairs of the persons and the property of Indians is preventing them from accommodating themselves to the conditions and requirements of modern life and from exercising that liberty with respect to their own affairs without which they cannot develop into self-reliant, free, and independent citizens and have the right which belongs generally to citizens of the United States; and

Whereas numerous complaints have been made by responsible persons and organizations charging improper and improvident administration of Indian property by the Bureau of Indian Affairs; and

Whereas it is claimed that preventable diseases are widespread among the Indian population, that the death rate among them is not only unreasonably high but is increasing, and that the Indians in many localities are becoming pauperized; and

Whereas the acts passed by Congress in the last hundred years having as their objective the civilization of the Indian tribes seem to have failed to accomplish the results anticipated; and

Whereas it is expedient that said acts of Congress and the Indian policy incorporated in said acts be examined and the administration and operation of the same as affecting the condition of the Indian population be surveyed and appraised: Now, therefore, be it

Resolved, That the Committee on Indian Affairs of the Senate is authorized and directed to make a general survey of the conditions of the Indians and of the operation and effect of the laws which Congress has passed for the civilization and protection of the Indian tribes; to investigate the relation of the Bureau of Indian Affairs to the persons and property of Indians and the effect of the acts, regulations, and administration of said bureau upon the health, improvements, and welfare of the Indians; and to report its findings in the premises, together with recommendations for the correction of abuses that may be found to exist, and for such changes in the law as will promote the security, economic competence, and progress of the Indians.

Said committee is authorized to send for persons, books, and papers, to administer oaths, to employ such clerical assistance as is necessary, to sit during any recess of the Senate, and at such places as it may deem advisable. Any subcommittee, duly authorized thereto, shall have the powers conferred upon the committee by this resolution.

The expenses of said investigation shall be paid out by the contingent fund of the Senate and shall not exceed $30,000.[10]

In this one resolution the Congress of the United States exposes the wound that has been unattended for so many decades. The complications enumerated have developed through lack of responsible care.

From the date of this survey began the reforms in regard to the status of the Indians that we know of in late years.

FOOTNOTES

[1] Felix S. Cohen, Handbook of Federal Indian Law (Washington, D.C.: U.S. Government Printing Office, 1942), p. 169.

[2] Cherokee Nation v. Georgia, 5 Pet. 1, 17, 18-20 (1831), pp. 17-18, 20.

[3] Chauncey Shafter Goodrich, "The Legal Status of the California Indian," California Law Review, XV (1926), 97.

[4] Ibid., p. 89.

[5] Brader v. James, 246 U.S. 88 (1918); Tiger v. Western Investment Co., 221 U.S. 286 (1911).

[6] N.C. Houghton, "The Legal Status of Indian Suffrage in the United States," California Law Review, XIX (1931), 507-518.

[7] F.S. Cohen, "Indian Rights and the Federal Courts," Minnesota Law Review, XXIV (1939-40), 149.

[8] U.S. v. Rickert, 188 U.S. 432, 445 (1903).

[9] Office of Indian Affairs, Circular No. 1665, April 26, 1921. Supplement to Circular No. 1665, February 14, 1923.

[10] Committee on Indian Affairs, The Problem of Indian Administration, Resolution 79, 70th Cong., 1st sess.

CHAPTER VI

LEGAL STATUS OF THE INDIAN SINCE THE

REORGANIZATION ACT OF 1934

In 1933 John Collier was appointed United States Commissioner of Indian Affairs. At long last the Indians had a true friend in a high place of power. He used this highest administrative office to improve the lot of his friends all over the United States. He realized that in the time of the existence of the United States there had been changes in all ways of life vaster than all changes that preceded that time in past history. The Indian from his primitive state was not able to proceed to a level of civilization equal to that of the white man. John Collier was supremely impressed with the fact that beyond the border between the United States and Mexico the proportion of Indians to whites is as great as the proportion of whites to Indians is on the north side of the border. The thirty million Indians of Mexico, Central, and South America are growing in population, education, and world power. These peoples to the south are watching the United States to see how it will treat this growing minority in its midst. Collier said what he hoped to accomplish during his term of appointment in an address on December 4, 1939.

What I describe shall be a bad beginning which lasted a long time, which broke Indian hearts for generation after generation, which inflicted destructions that no future time can wholly repair. Then I shall describe how the long-lasting bad record was changed to something good; how, although the change came so late, it did not come too late; how when the change came, it still found hundreds of Indian tribes ready to respond to the opportunity which had at last been given them. I shall describe how the good change has developed across three Presidencies, so that it is not an achievement or program of a single political party.[1]

Commissioner Collier set certain goals for progress in the development of the Indians to a place of self-sufficiency and self-respect. His policies were aimed at restoring the Indian to his rightful place in the galaxy of peoples. He knew how the allotment system had played havoc with the Indian lands. Collier illustrated the certain things that had to be done and the Indians put their faith once again in a white man; but this time they placed faith and trust in a white man who deserved it and did not betray their faith and trust. Through voluntary exchanges and relinquishing of rights of the many heirs involved in heirship cases some gain has been made in stemming the tide of damage done by the Allotment Act. The land that has been lost can not be gotten back unless purchased. A regathering and holding of the land in tribal or corporate unit was an aim of Collier's policy. All forms of white society have their credit unions and credit agencies, and one must be set up for the Indians, reasoned the Commissioner. This credit to buy know-how in the setting up of agricultural projects, stopping land erosion, and training of men in the use of modern equipment of all kinds, was a commendable project.

For many years the forced attendance of Indian children at the day schools set up in the larger white communities of the southwest was a sore spot with the Indians. The children were being taken from their family circles and shipped to a school from which they were not allowed to return until their term was over. Their culture was wrested from them, and their taboos ignored, or worse--ridiculed. Only a few children could be reached by the method of boarding schools. Day schools were needed on the reservations where children could come and gain occupationally useful knowledge and practice. It was Commissioner Collier's hope to establish schools for Indian children that needed institutional care; also he hoped to work in adult education on the reservation. If his policies could be put into practice they would be felt by every Indian on reservation in the realms of health, education, recreation, and welfare.

A policy that had been the dream of the Commissioner when he was teaching school in California and other states of the southwest was the decentralizing of the Indian Bureau. He believed that the Indian Service could only function when it came into daily contact with Indian life. He dreamed of an integration of the Indian Service with co-operating federal agencies, states, counties, school districts, municipalities, irrigation districts, and any other organized forms which could help the Indian to live a normal life by the white man's standards.

Today there are as many Indians working in the Indian Service as there are whites. In 1910 there were only 200 Indians in the employ of the Office of Indian Affairs; in 1937 there were 6,933 permanent employees. More than 40 per cent of the Indians employed were full-blooded Indians. This was a policy of John Collier. He worked hard for adjustments to be made in Civil Service procurement programs and methods so that Indians could be given the opportunity to perform the duties entailed in the administration of all facets of the Indian Bureau of Affairs. Care had to be taken that standards were not lowered in the adjustments so he sought grants to aid in the professional training of Indians to fill the positions that appeared on the lists. With the decentralization of Indian administration to tribal headquarters on the several reservations more and more of the unofficial work has been turned over to the members of the tribe who are most capable of doing the work.

Prior to 1934 very little effort had been made by the Indian Bureau to get the ideas of the Indians on legislation they desired for their own benefit. When the Indian Reorganization Bill of 1934 was being promulgated the assistance of the Indians was sought in the form of questionnaires. They were asked what were the main problems which they faced. Before submitting the bill[2] copies were sent to the various tribes and round table discussions were held to evaluate the merit of the bill. The original form of the bill had the following parts:

1. The Indian societies were to be recognized, and be empowered and helped to undertake political, administrative and economic self-government.

2. Provision was made for an Indian civil service and for the training of Indians in administration, the professions and other vocations.

3. Land allotment was to be stopped, and the revestment of Indians with land was provided for.

4. A system of agricultural and industrial credit was to be established, and the needed funds authorized.

5. Civil and criminal law enforcement, below the level reached by federal court jurisdiction, was to be set up under a system of courts operating with simplified procedures and ultimately responsible to the tribes.

6. The consolidation of fractionalized allotted lands, and the delivery of allotments back into the tribal estate, was provided for under conditions which safeguarded all individual property rights and freedoms. [3]

The last two parts were not incorporated in the law as finally passed by Congress. That the last was not passed is considered to be a major disaster which Congress has not yet repaired. Indian land was fractionalized by the General Allotment Act and over ninety million acres of reservation land lost by the Indians from 1887 to 1933, and the use of most of the rest was lost to the use of white men. Under the Allotment Act each little plot of land has an innumerable number of heirs, and one Indian may have the vesting of as many as fifty heirship equities. The heirs to one fraction of land may be scattered across the forty-eight states. As late as December, 1944, this problem was presented to the House Sub-Committee on Indian Investigation. As yet our government has taken no direct stand nor action on this problem.

John Collier and his organization began at once to implement the policies so long dreamed of by him and given the go ahead by the <u>Reorganization Act of 1934.</u> The regeneration and freeing of Indian societies and the training in a democratic way of life has been carried on space. There have been many shortcomings on the part of the Indian Bureau, but the good which has been accomplished since 1933 far outweighs even the intended good accomplished for 160 years before that date.

Some of the shortcomings on the part of the Bureau have not been the fault of the administration, but reflect the bitterness that is still felt on the reservations as a result of over a century and a half of slaughter and starvation. As a direct result of the Reorganization Act more than a hundred tribes adopted constitutions and inaugurated self-government. Most of the regulations of the administrative offices in the Indian Service are so constructed that they can be adapted to the particular tribe in accordance with that tribe's constitution and by-laws. It is now recognized, and practiced, that the government agencies are dealing with groups of peoples who have different economic ideologies, political organizations, and widely differentiated as to standard of living. The tribal governments which are set up under the various constitutions naturally are manned with Indian leaders who mirror the latent bitterness of the Indians after the years of heartbreak.

Tribal unity and organization is in a position to pool resources and grievances and hire counsel to enforce governmental recognition of rights. In California the Indian Council has instituted several successful suits against the United States since the passage of the <u>Reorganization Act.</u> Never will the courts of the United States, no matter how lenient with money, be able to quench the fires which burn so brilliantly as a result of rivers of Indian blood unnecessarily shed.

Incidentally, in 1938, the Court of Claims awarded the Klamath Indians over five million dollars.[4] The inescapable truth would seem to be that our government is ready to admit mistakes and make restitution for at least some of the errors of past generations.

The Indians now are having their day in court. They have received the benefit of excellent counsel. Decisions in the Federal Courts in recent years favor the Indian. Over and over again the courts reiterate the fact that Indians are citizens and are entitled to all the rights to which non-Indians are entitled under the statutes and codes of the United States.

On April 28, 1934, President F. D. Roosevelt stated in a message urging passage of the Wheeler-Howard Act (Reorganization Act);

> The Wheeler-Howard bill embodies the basic and broad principles of the administration for a new standard of dealing between the Federal Government and its Indian wards.
>
> It is, in the main, a measure of justice that is long overdue.
>
> We can and should, without further delay, extend to the Indian the fundamental rights of political liberty and local self-government and the opportunities of education and economic assistance that they require in order to obtain a wholesome American life. This is but the obligation of honor of a powerful nation toward a people living among us and dependent upon our protection.
>
> Certainly the continuance of autocratic rule, by a federal department, over the lives of more than 200,000 citizens of this Nation is incompatible with American ideals of liberty. It also is destructive of the character and self-respect of a great race.
>
> The continued application of the allotment laws, under which Indian wards have lost more than two-thirds of their reservation lands, while the costs of Federal administration of these lands have steadily mounted, must be terminated.
>
> Indians throughout the country have been stirred to a new hope. They say they stand at the end of the old trail. Certainly, the figures of impoverishment and disease point to their impending extinction, as a race, unless basic changes in their conditions of life are effected.
>
> I do not think such changes can be devised and carried out without the active cooperation of the Indians themselves.
>
> The Wheeler-Howard bill offers the basis for such cooperation. It allows the Indian people to take an active and responsible part in the solution of their own problems. [5]

From 1884 to November 27, 1935, regulations in force on the Indian reservations had given the agents powers of police, prosecutor, jury, judge, and warden. At the request of John Collier, Secretary of the Interior Harold Ickes revoked the powers of the agents. The whole system of law and order on the reservations was turned over to the tribes and groups. Commissioner Collier described the new look in Indian judiciary as a great step toward elimination of injustices on the reservations. Regulations are now modified to fit the requirements of each tribe organized under the Indian Reorganization Act. The individual tribes have been given greater powers in dealing with male factors in their midst. Officials of the Indian Service are not permitted to interfere with the functions of the Indian courts. Now the offenses are enumerated and the fines and punishments listed. [6]

This ended the concentration of power in one man who was answerable to a central government so far away that the cries of the oppressed have only occasionally reached the government. In illustration of the arbitrary quality of the agency system one agent wrote to the Bureau that there was no trouble on his reservation of amongst the Indians under his jurisdiction, because he punished them as he saw fit and the Indians never offered resistance. It is almost unbelievable that in this modern and enlightened day hundreds of thousands of human beings could have suffered oppression within the boundaries of the United States.

Felix S. Cohen proves one fact in this monumental work on the federal laws relating to the Indians. That fact is the Indian of the United States is a citizen of the United States today. All of the Indians in the United States are entitled to all of the rights to which the white man is entitled. The enactment on June 2, 1924, of a bill providing for the citizenship status of all non-citizen Indians born within the territorial limits of the United States left no doubt as to the citizenship status of the Indian before the eyes of the federal government. When an Indian of the Pima Tribe attempted to register to vote in Pinal County, Arizona, the right was refused him by the county registrar. The courts held that no one should participate in the making of laws which he need not obey. It was further decided that the reservation Indian could not vote because:

1. Reservation Indians were not residents of the State;

2. held persons under guardianship;

3. Indians on the reservation not subject to the laws of the state for action or conduct on reservation. [7]

The reason the several states refused the right of suffrage to the Indians living within their boundaries on reservations stems from the fact that we have mentioned earlier in this study, that the individual is answerable to the tribe and the tribe to the federal government. The states feel that they are losing out by not being able to tax and control the people on, and the land of, the reservations. [8]

With all of the constitutional amendments guaranteeing freedom and equality which are found in the fifth, fourteenth, and fifteenth amendments; and the various laws which provide stiff penalties for discrimination against other men because of their race, color, and creed, the Indians are still discriminated against. Several acts have stated that all Indians not already citizens are now citizens. The tribes have been given rights over the Individuals as far as law, taxation, membership, and domestic relations are concerned. But the actual Indian affairs in and out of the tribe, and off and on the reservation, are controlled by the federal government under authority vested in it through application of the clause of the Constitution of the United States which states that the Congress of the United States has the power "to regulate commerce with the Indian tribes." Difficulties which have arisen from the application of this clause have been aggravated by misunderstanding of the legal position of Indians. The Indians do occupy a unique place in the international relationship existing between them and the United States. Complexities arising from the multitude of treaties, statutes, judicial opinions, and less authoritative writings have bewildered Indians to such an extent that many of them do not believe they are citizens. Judge Cuthbert Pound has pointed out that all attempts to "lay down certain simple rules of alleged universal applicability" for the legal status of the Indians have failed. Judge Pound says that many citizens believe that Indians, as "ward Indians," do not have any capacity to make contracts or to bring or defend law suits.[9]

The act of June 2, 1924 (43 Stat. 253, 8 U.S.C. 3) naturalized 125,000 native-born Indians with one stroke of the pen. The provision of this act was:

> That all non-citizen Indians born within the territorial limits of the United States be, and they are hereby, declared to be citizens of the United States: Provided, That the granting of such citizenship shall not in any manner impair or otherwise affect the right of any Indian to tribal or other property.[10]

This provision was incorporated into the Nationality Act of October 14, 1940 which states:

> The right to become a naturalized citizen under the provisions of this Act shall extend only to white persons, persons of African nativity or descent, and descendants of races indigenous to the Western Hemisphere.

This legislation had the obvious purpose of excluding the peoples of the Orient from becoming citizens of the United States.

Indians had acquired citizenship through specific treaties which named members of entire tribes or groups as citizens of the United States. Laws had been passed by Congress, such as the Act of May 2, 1890, which specified that:

> . . . any member of any Indian tribe or nation residing in the Indian Territory may apply to the United States court therein to become a citizen of the United States, and such court shall have jurisdiction thereof and shall hear and determine such application as provided in the statutes of the United States . . . . Provided, that the Indians who become citizens of the United States under the provisions of this Act do not forfeit or lose any rights or privileges they enjoy or are entitled to as members of the tribe or nation to which they belong.[11]

Almost at any time in our history, after the mid-nineteenth century point was passed, an Indian who could read, write, and speak English could obtain citizenship upon request. An Indian who could use the English language and who lived apart from a reservation could obtain citizenship upon the adoption of the habits of civilization. Indian women who married citizens obtained citizenship through the Act of August 9, 1888. The Indian men who, although not citizens prior to enlistment, enlisted for duty in World War I could obtain citizenship through utilization of the Act of November 6, 1919. Citizenship is important if the individual desires the right of suffrage. According to the California State Constitution of 1879, Article II, section 1, "Every native citizen of the United States . . . shall be entitled to vote at all elections. . . ." On July 15, 1948, the Supreme Court of Arizona declared the Indians of that state were not "under guardianship" and now were able to vote. On August 3, 1948, three judges in the Santa Fe, New Mexico, Federal Court ruled that New Mexico had been in error to keep the 20,000 eligible Indians from voting on the grounds of being Indians "not taxed." In the court fights previous to the 1948 battles, Indians would be forced to withdraw at the moment of hearing for fear of reprisals. This time the cases were taken all the way by veterans of World War II who had such legal aid as could be supplied by the Department of Justice of the United States, the Department of the Interior, Chief Counsel James E. Curry, and the dean of Indian lawyers, Felix S. Cohen. With the overwhelming force brought to bear in Arizona, the Supreme Court of that state held the Indians eligible to vote. The decision stated:

> In a democracy suffrage is the most basic civil right, since its exercise is the chief means whereby other rights may be safeguarded. To deny the right to vote, where one is legally entitled to do so, is to do violence to the principles of freedom and equality . . . . We have made an extensive search of the proceedings of the Arizona Constitutional Convention and are unable to find the slightest evidence to indicate that the framers . . . in specifying that "persons under guardianship" . . . should be denied the right of franchise . . . intended that

phrase be applied to Indians as such. The same thing may be said as to the legislative implementing enactment . . . . In other words, the legislative department has not set up this barrier; rather we feel it is a tortuous construction by the Judicial branch . . . accomplishing a purpose . . . never designed by its framers.

Judges Phillips of Colorado, and Bower Breaddus and Royce H. Savage of Oklahoma, were appointed to hear the case held in Santa Fe. They found that the defense of the veteran who had asked for the injunction of re-strainer on the registrar of voters was an attack on the constitutional provi-sion disqualifying "Indians not taxed." The lawyers pointed out that Indians pay income taxes, sales taxes, excise taxes, automobile taxes, gasoline taxes, all taxes paid by any inhabitant with the single exception of ad valorem taxes on real property held in trust for them by the United States Government. The judges found that the New Mexico statute contravenes the 15th Amend-ment which states "the right of citizens of the United States to vote shall not be denied or abridged by the United States or by any state on account of race, color, or previous condition of servitude." The court further ruled that the portions of the New Mexico Constitution and enabling act which denied the right of Indians to vote are unconstitutional and void. They went to the ex-tent of declaring that no Indian shall hereafter be disqualified from voting on the ground that he is an "Indian not taxed."[12]

Before the Allotment Act of 1887 the Indians had only a right of occu-pancy with the United States Government holding the title to the land. Later the Indians were placed on reservations that delivered no right of title to the Indians living thereon. After the Allotment Act the tribes not specifically named in the Act had their lands split up and small portions given to indivi-dual members of the tribe. The federal government was to keep title in the land for twenty-five years. This was a trust sort of deal in which the allottee would obtain title after the twenty-five years were up, if the government did not decide to extend the length of the period. All this time the Indian was not to have relationships with the state in which the reservation upon which he lived was geographically located. He had no right to pay real estate taxes on land held under the Allotment Act, nor could he avail himself of the public schools, health facilities, and other organized divisions for health, education and welfare. The federal government has kept the land of the Indian, and declared it inalienable so that the Indian in his improvidence and ignorance would not lose what he had left. The sorest spot in the whole picture in so far as the several states are concerned is the non-payment of taxes by the Indians. If the land was alienable then taxes would be assessed and over a period of time the non-payment of taxes would deliver the Indian's land into the hands of the state. Congress made it permissible for an executive officer to extend the time of alienation restriction originally put on the land by act of Congress. What happened so often was that an Indian would obtain his patent in fee simple and then, under the Burke Act of May 8, 1906, he would gain citizenship. According to legal ideology the Indian had gained competency by obtaining his patent. He would then alienate his land for enough money or other value to keep him for a short time after which he would be without land or means of any kind. This did much to hurt the individuals working for the welfare of the Indians.[13]

The promulgators of the California State Constitution made it mandatory upon the legislature to pass laws establishing free common schools. Ratification of the constitution by the people of California placed the responsibility of educating the children of California upon the people. The California courts have declared that general systems of education were distinctly a state affair.[14] Even if Indian children live on a reservation the local school district may not deny them admission.[15] It is further held that Indian children may choose between near-by Federal Indian Schools or local public schools. The Compulsory Education Law (Stats. [1921], p. 1673) prescribed alternative systems of schooling, but it is pointed out therein that this act was for the exercise of a free volition and was not intended as a denial of the right to attend public schools.

Another factor which has evolved in the favor of the Indians of the United States and the State of California is the application to them of the Social Security Act. The Solicitor for the Department of Interior, Mr. David Margold, in a memorandum dated April 22, 1936, held that the Social Security Act was applicable to Indians. The Solicitor went on to state his reasoning behind the memorandum. An Indian votes or is entitled to vote.[16] Indian children are entitled to attend public schools, and this notwithstanding the availability of a Federal Indian School.[17] The Indian may sue and be sued in State courts, and his ordinary contracts and engagements are subject to state law.[18] When the Indian is off the reservation his personal conduct is subject to state law. He is not exempt from any of the taxes which reach the rest of the population such as sales tax and all non-trust property which he may own and all fees and taxes for the enjoyment of state privileges. When the taxes paid by Indians are insufficient to support state Indian schools, hospitals, and other projects the Federal Government uses trust or tribal funds to defray the expenses.[19] Indians are constantly receiving care in state institutions either without charge or with payment from their own outside resources. In the absence of a specific old age pension system, or any general provision for the Indians, the qualified American Indian is subject to the benefits of the Social Security Act.[20]

FOOTNOTES

[1] Felix S. Cohen, Handbook of Federal Indian Law, op. cit., Introduction.

[2] Also known as the Wheeler-Howard Act.

[3] John Collier, Indians of the Americas, The Long Hope (New York: A Mentor Book, 1947), p. 157.

[4]Cohen, "Original Indian Title," Minnesota Law Review, XXXII (1948), p. 38.

[5]Cohen, Handbook of Federal Indian Law.

[6]Felix S. Cohen, "Indian Rights and the Federal Courts," Minnesota Law Review, XXIV (1940), 145.

[7]Porter v. Hall (1928), 24 Ariz. 308, 271 Pac. 411.

[8]N. D. Houghton, "The Legal Status of Indian Suffrage in the United States," California Law Review, XIX (1930-1931), 507-520.

[9]Judge Cuthbert Pound, "Nationals without a Nation," Colorado Law Review, XXII (1922), 97.

[10]Hon. Hubert Work, Indian Policies: Comments on Resolutions of the Advisory Council on Indian Affairs (Washington, D.C.: U.S. Government Printing Office, 1924).

[11]Act of May 2, 1890, sec. 43, 26 Stat. 81, 99-100.

[12]Henry Christman, "Southwestern Indians Win the Vote," The American Indian, IV (1948).

[13]Felix S. Cohen, "Indian Rights and the Federal Courts," loc. cit.; and, "Original Indian Titles," Minnesota Law Review, XXXII.

[14]Peters v. Pauma School District, 91 Cal. 792, 267 P 576.

[15]Piper v. Big Pine School District, 193 Cal. 664, 672.

[16]Anderson v. Mathews, 174 Cal. 537, 163 Pac. 902.

[17]Piper v. Big Pine School District, 193 Cal. 664, 226 Pac. 926.

[18]Luigi Marre & Cattle Co. v. Roses, 34 P, (2) 195 (Cal. 1934).

[19]Decisions of the Comptroller of the Treasury 678.

[20]Cohen, Handbook of Federal Indian Law, op. cit., p. 162.

CHAPTER VII

CONCLUSION

The Spanish Crown decreed that the Indians should be accorded equal rights as subjects of Castile. The Mexican Government after 1821 decreed that the Indians should have equality with the white man. Five thousand laws and statutes between the United States, the several states, and the Indians have decreed how the Indian was to be treated. Until 1933 the problems which plagued the Indian-white relationships went from bad to worse. Since 1933 there has been a distinct endeavor to incorporate the Indian into the white man's society.

Under the impetus of the Indian Reorganization Act the Indian tribes in many areas are forging ahead rapidly. The tribes who have taken advantage of incorporation are organizing under new chieftains elected for educational background and ability to lead their tribes into the new way of life. As soon as circumstances will permit the United States Government plans to eliminate the Indian Bureau and leave the problems which may arise with regard to the Indians up to the several states and local governments. In California the majority of the Indians wish for this withdrawal, but not until many financial problems are taken care of first.

It is too early to pass conclusive judgment on the progress being made toward integration of the Indian into white society. Where the individual Indian has left the Indian reservation and the Indian way of life to adopt the white man's ways, the transition is usually successful. Perhaps the programs which have been initiated in the past few years and the de-segregation court decisions will mend the damage done by decades of close segregation.

BIBLIOGRAPHY

A. Books

Bancroft, Hubert Howe. History of California. San Francisco: A. L. Bancroft & Company, Publishers, 1884. 5 vols.

Barber, Ruth Kerns. Indian Labor in the Spanish Colonies. New Mexico: University of New Mexico Press, 1932.

Bernstein, Harry. Modern and Contemporary Latin America. Chicago: J. B. Lippincott Co., 1952.

Blumenthal, Walter Hart. American Indians Dispossessed. Philadelphia: George S. MacManus Co., 1955.

Browne, J. R. The Indians of California. San Francisco: Colt Press, 1944.

Caughey, John W. California. New York: Prentice-Hall, Inc., 1953. 666 pp.

Chapman, Charles Edward. California, The Spanish Period. New York: The Macmillan Company, 1939. 527 pp.

Clark, George. Indians of Yosemite Valley and Vicinity. Yosemite: George Clark Press, 1907.

Cohen, Felix S. Handbook of Federal Indian Law. Washington: U.S. Government Printing Office, 1942. 662 pp.

Collier, John. Indians of the Americas, The Long Hope. New York: A Mentor Book, 1947. 191 pp.

Dale, Everett Edward. The Indians of the Southwest. Norman: The University of Oklahoma Press, 1949.

Eastman, Charles Alexander. The Indian Today. New York: Doubleday, Page & Co., 1915.

Ellison, William Henry. A Self-Governing Dominion: California, 1849-1860. Berkeley: University of California Press, 1950.

Hittell, T. H. <u>History of California.</u> 1897. 5 vols.

Hoopes, Alban W. <u>Indian Affairs and Their Administration, with Special Reference to the Far West, 1849-1860.</u> Philadelphia: 1932.

Hunt, Rockwell D. <u>A Short History of California.</u> New York: Thomas Y. Crowell Co., 1929.

Kroeber, A. L. <u>Handbook of the Indians of California.</u> Berkeley: California Book Company, Ltd., 1953. 995 pp.

Pancost, Henry Spackman. <u>The Indian before the Law.</u> Philadelphia: Printed by order of the executive committee of the Indian Rights Association, 1884.

Prescott, William Hickling. <u>Isabel I, la Catolica, Queen of Spain, 1451-1504.</u> Boston: C.C. Little & J. Brown, 1846.

Priestley, Herbert Ingram. <u>Jose de Galvez, Visitor-General of New Spain, 1765-1771.</u> Berkeley, California: University of California Press, 1916.

_____. <u>The Mexican Nation, A History.</u> New York: The Macmillan Co., 1930.

Royce, Charles C. <u>Indian Land Cessions in the United States.</u> Washington: Smithsonian Institute Reports, 1899.

Simpson, Eyler N. <u>The Ejido--Mexico's Way Out.</u> Chapel Hill: Duke University Press, 1937.

Simpson, Lesley Byrd. <u>Encomienda in New Spain.</u> Berkeley: University of California Press, 1950.

_____. <u>Exploitation of Land in Central Mexico in the 16th Century.</u> Berkeley: University of California Press, 1952.

_____. <u>Many Mexicos.</u> New York: Putnam, 1941.

Thomas, Alfred Barnaby. <u>Teodoro de Croix and the Northern Frontier of New Spain, 1776-1783.</u> Oklahoma: University of Oklahoma Press, 1941.

B. Publications of the Government, Learned Societies, and Other Organizations

Abbott, Austin. "Indians and the Law," Harvard Law Review, II, 167, 175-6.

Abbott, Lyman. "Our Indian Problem," North American Review, 167 (1898), 721-3.

Brown, Robert C. "The Taxation of Indian Property," Minnesota Law Review, XV (1930-31).

Christman, Henry. "Southwestern Indians Win the Vote," The American Indian, IV (1948).

Cohen, Felix S. "Indian Rights and the Federal Courts," Minnesota Law Review, XXIV (1939-40), 145-200.

_____. "Original Indian Title," Minnesota Law Review, XXXII (1947-48).

Compiled Laws of the State of California Passed at Sessions of 1850-51-52-53, compiled by S. Garfielde. Bencia: Garfielde, 1853.

Congressional globe, 35th Cong., 2nd sess., Pt. 1, pp. 694, 734-735; U.S. Stat., 25th Cong., 2nd sess., p. 400; Congressional globe, 36th Cong., 1st sess., Pt. 3, pp. 2368-2369, Pt. 4, p. 2904; U.S. Stat., 26th Cong., 1st sess., p. 57.

Ellison, William H. "The Federal Indian Policy in California, 1846-1860," Mississippi Valley Historical Review, IX (June, 1922), 1.

Goodrich, Chauncey Shafter. "The Legal Status of the California Indian," California Law Review, XIV (1926), 83-100, 157-200.

Hornblower, W.B. "The Legal Status of the Indians," Reports of the American Bar Association, XIV (1891), 261.

Houghton, N.D. "The Legal Status of Indian Suffrage in the United States," California Law Review, XIX (1930-1931), 507-20.

Kappler, Charles J. Indian Affairs, U.S. Laws, Statutes . . . Washington: U.S. Government Printing Office, 1903.

Mudgett, Helen Parker. Indian Tribes and Treaties, A Regional Conference Report. Minneapolis, Minnesota: University of Minnesota, April 23-24, 1955.

Padover, J.P.   "The Complete Jefferson," Minnesota Law Review, XXXII
        (1947).

Priestley, Herbert Ingraham.   "Spanish Colonial Municipalities," California
        Law Review, (1919), 397-416.

"Program for the Termination of Indian Bureau Activities in the State of
        California." Prepared by the California Indian Agency, Sacramento
        California; submitted to the Commissioner of Indian Affairs, June,
        1949. [Mimeographed]

"Progress Report to the Legislature by the Senate Interim Committee on Cal-
        ifornia Indian Affairs." Senate Resolution No. 115. Sacramento,
        California: Published by the Senate of the State of California, 1955.

Thayer, Ezra Ripley [compiler].   Legal Essays of James Bradley Thayer.
        Cambridge: Harvard University Press, 1927.

Thayer, James B.   "A People without Law," Atlantic Monthly, LXVIII, 681.

Wise, J.C.   "Indian Law and Needed Reforms," American Bar Association
        Journal, XII (January, 1926), 38.

_____.   "A Plea for the Indian Citizens of the United States." Washington:
        V, Congressional Record of December 15, 1925.

Work, Hubert.   Indian Policies: Comments on Resolutions of the Advisory
        Council on Indian Affairs. Washington: U.S. Government Printing
        Office, 1924.

                            C. Legal Cases

Anderson v. Mathews, 174 Cal. 537, 542-4.

Apapas v. U.S. (1914), 233 U.S. 587, 590, 58 L. Ed. 1104, 34 Sup. Ct.
        Rep. 704.

Cherokee Nation v. Georgia, 5 Peters 1.

Conners v. U.S. et al., 33 C. cls., 317 (1898).

Cramer v. U.S., 261 U.S. 219, 233.

Fletcher v. Peck, 6 Cranch 87-142.

Francisco v. IAC, 192 Cal. 635, 639-41.

Hallowell v. U.S. (1911), 221 U.S. 317, 324, 55 L. Ed. 750, 31 Supr. Ct.
Rep. 587.

In Matter of Heff (1905), 197 U.S. 488, 508-9, 49 L. Ed. 848, 25 Supr. Ct.
Rep. 506.

Johnson v. McIntosh, 8 Wheaton 574.

Jones v. Meehan (1899), 175 U.S. 1.

Lone Wolf v. Hitchcock (1903), 187 U.S. 553, 564, 47 L. Ed. 299, 23
Sup. Ct. Rep. 216.

In re Look Tin Sing, 21 Fed. 905, 909.

Luigi Marre & Cattle Co. v. Roses, 34 P. (2) 195 Cal. 1934.

People v. Bray, 105 Cal. 344, 347.

Peters v. Pauma School District of San Diego City, 91 Cal. 792, 267, p. 576.

Piper v. Big Pine School District, 193 Cal. 664, 672.

Porter v. Hall (1928), 24 Ariz. 308, 271 Pac. 411.

Tiger v. Western Inv. Co. (1911), 221 U.S. 286, 315, 55 L. Ed. 738, 31
Sup. Ct. Rep. 578.

Winter v. Amos (1921), 255 U.S. 373, 392, 65 L. Ed. 684, 41 Sup. Ct.
Rep. 342.

Worcester v. Georgia, 6 Peters 515.

U.S. v. Kagama, 118 U.S. 375, 383-4.

U.S. v. Noble, (1915), 237 U.S. 587, 590, 58 L. Ed. 1104, 34 Sup. Ct. Rep.
532.

U.S. v. Pearson (1916), 231 Fed. 270.

U.S. v. Rickert (1903), 188 U.S. 432, 47 L. Ed. 532, 23 Sup. Ct. Rep. 478.

U.S. v. Ritchie, 58 U.S. 525, 538.

U.S. v. Rogers, 4 How. 567 (1846).

U.S. v. Sandoval (1913), 231 U.S. 28, 48, 58 L. Ed. 107, Sup. Ct. Rep. 1.

U.S. v. Santistevan, 1 N.M., 583, 591.

U.S. ex rel. Standing Bear v. Crook, (CC Nev. 1879), 5 Dill 453, 25 Fed.
    Cas. No. 14, 891.

U.S. v. Waller, 243 U.S. 452, 459.